Business Insights on Emerging Markets 2024

OECD DEVELOPMENT CENTRE

EM»net OECD EMERGING MARKETS NETWORK

Please cite this publication as:
OECD (2024), *Business Insights on Emerging Markets 2024*, OECD Publishing, Paris, https://doi.org/10.1787/7d6b7375-en.

ISBN 978-92-64-90952-6 (print)
ISBN 978-92-64-57614-8 (PDF)
ISBN 978-92-64-46519-0 (HTML)
ISBN 978-92-64-75683-0 (epub)

Business Insights on Emerging Markets
ISSN 3007-9381 (online)

Photo credits: Cover design by Aida Buendia, OECD Development Centre.

Corrigenda to OECD publications may be found at: https://www.oecd.org/en/publications/support/corrigenda.html.

Acknowledgements

This publication was prepared by the Organisation for Economic Co-operation and Development (OECD) Development Centre's Emerging Markets Network (EMnet); it includes a chapter from the Emerging Markets Institute of the Samuel Curtis Johnson College of Business at Cornell University. Bathylle Missika and Lorenzo Pavone, Head and Deputy Head, respectively, of the Networks, Partnerships and Gender Division, guided the project. The publication was developed by Edoardo Cozzi and Majda Eddaifi, Policy Analysts. It received inputs from Francisca Faden and Gabriela Jimenez Echeverri, EMnet Trainees.

The opening chapter, "Trends in foreign direct investment into emerging markets", was prepared by Edoardo Cozzi, Francisca Faden and Gabriela Jimenez Echeverri.

Chapter 2, "Private sector insights on emerging markets", was drafted by Edoardo Cozzi and Majda Eddaifi. The chapter captures insights from the EMnet meetings held in 2023, including the Working Group on Business and Sustainability (6 April, Paris), the Working Group on Digital Transformation (14 April, Washington DC), the Business Meeting on Latin America (6 June, Paris), the Business Meeting on Economic Resilience and Green Transition (4 October, Costa Rica), the Business Meeting on Africa (30 October, Paris), the EMnet Webinar at OECD COP 28 Virtual Pavilion (28 November). The meetings featured the participation of high-level policy makers, senior business executives and OECD experts. Further insights originate from desk research and bilateral conversations with EMnet members and other multinational companies operating in emerging markets. DHL, Mastercard, MUFG Bank, and Telefonica contributed through their review and additional comments to sharpen the analysis.

Chapter 3, "Central Banks Digital Currencies (CBDCs): What is in it for Emerging Markets", was written by Lourdes S. Casanova, Academic Director, Anne Miroux, Faculty Fellow, and Sharwari Pandit, Research Fellow, respectively of the Emerging Markets Institute of the Samuel Curtis Johnson College of Business at Cornell University.

The chapters benefited from comments and inputs from the following experts: Arthur Minsat, Kensuke Molnar-Tanaka, Sebastian Nieto Parra, Ana Novik, Fares Al Hussami, Marie-Estelle Rey, Alexander Böhmer, Karim Dahou, Tamas Hajba, Nejla Saula, Ferre Westermann (OECD).

Finally, the team is very grateful to the OECD Development Centre's Communications and Publications Unit, especially Delphine Grandrieux and Elizabeth Nash, for its support in producing this publication, as well as the copy editor Gemma Nellies. The authors also thank Henri-Bernard Solignac-Lecomte, Aida Buendía, Rebecca Appel and Felix Zimmermann of the OECD Development Centre's Communications and Publications Unit for their contributions. Finally, special thanks go to Sonja Märki, Anita Buzas, Sabrina Bouldi and Esme Stout, Partnerships and Gender Division (OECD Development Centre) for their valuable assistance throughout the drafting and publishing process.

Editorial

In a world beset by geopolitical tensions and economic uncertainty, emerging markets closed 2023 with robust growth rates. This momentum has carried into 2024, with gross domestic product (GDP) growth exceeding expectations, inflation declining in most countries, and capital flows to emerging-market economies increasing over the past year. As we count down to 2030, it is crucial to understand the dynamics at play and harness opportunities to foster resilient and sustainable economic development.

Private investment is conducive to economic and social development in several important ways. Companies can help harness the benefits of the digital transition, by investing in research and development, connectivity and the reskilling of workers. Private investment in new technologies can also help emerging and developing countries accelerate the green transition and achieve climate change objectives. Between 2020 and 2023, multinational enterprises headquartered in OECD countries initiated around 75% of the new projects announced in emerging and developing economies and created over 3 million new jobs. For instance, in Latin America and the Caribbean (LAC), greenfield foreign direct investment (FDI) in renewable energy has surpassed fossil fuels almost without fail every year since 2011.

Moving forward, governments can encourage more private investment, by creating a sound business environment, strengthening the dialogue with investors and promoting the conditions for positive spillovers to local economies. In this context, the EMnet report *Business Insights on Emerging Markets* provides a valuable collection of the main dynamics, challenges and ways forward for the private sector operating in Africa, Asia and LAC.

Ambitious and successful policy reforms demand close collaboration between private and public sectors. On the one hand, emerging countries need innovative policies and regulations to create a more favourable environment for investment. This includes harmonising policies, enhancing regional integration, promoting competition and fostering regulatory stability. On the other hand, the private sector and governments must implement collaborative strategies, to collect and share data, promote sustainable business practices and maximise the positive impact of private investment on local communities. Such efforts are evidenced by the role of environmental, social and governance (ESG) investments, which in 2022 constituted 18% of foreign financing in emerging economies excluding the People's Republic of China.

The OECD Development Centre is grateful to its EMnet members for their active engagement and valuable contributions. Their support has enriched this new edition of the report, helping contribute to the Centre's overarching mission of promoting stronger, more inclusive, and greener development.

Ragnheiður Elín Árnadóttir

Director, OECD Development Centre

Table of contents

FIGURES

TABLES

BOXES

Abbreviations and acronyms

AfVIP	African Virtual Investment Platform
ASEAN	Association of Southeast Asian Nations
AUC	African Union Commission
CAPEX	company capital expenditure
CBDC	central bank digital currency
DREX	Digital Brazilian Real
EMnet	Emerging Markets Network
ESG	environmental, social and governance
FDI	foreign direct investment
GDP	gross domestic product
GSSS	green, social, sustainable and sustainability-linked
ICT	information and communication technology
LAC	Latin America and the Caribbean
MENA	Middle East and Northern Africa
MSMEs	micro, small and medium-sized enterprises
NFC	near-field communication
RBC	Responsible Business Conduct
RBI	Reserve Bank of India
SEZs	special economic zones
SIGI	Social Institutions and Gender Index
SMEs	small and medium-sized enterprises
UPI	Unified Payment Interface

Executive summary

Recent trends in emerging markets

The global economy has proved resilient against a backdrop of geopolitical tension and tighter monetary policies to counterbalance inflationary pressures. In 2023, emerging and developing economies exhibited robust growth rates, close to those observed prior to the COVID-19 pandemic. Emerging Asia is the world region predicted to experience the highest gross domestic product (GDP) increase in the period 2023-25, at 5.2% in 2024 and 4.8% in 2025. Latin America and Sub-Saharan Africa are predicted to grow respectively by 1.9% and 3.8% in 2024 and 2.5% and 4.1% in 2025.

Foreign direct investment (FDI) into emerging economies rebounded in 2021, although the positive momentum following the announcement of greenfield investments slowed down in the first six months of 2023 compared to the second half of 2022. In Africa, the potential of FDI to foster sustainable development remains largely untapped, primarily due to its limited integration into domestic productive activities. Latin America and the Caribbean (LAC) exhibits high FDI inflows, becoming the leading recipient of FDI relative to its GDP at 4% in 2021. Emerging Asia is predicted to remain attractive for FDI, thanks to competitive wages, increasing domestic demand, and improved business regulations and infrastructure.

Private sector insights on emerging markets

Throughout the year, member companies and partners participated in several initiatives organised by the OECD Emerging Markets Network, sharing insights to help policy makers in emerging markets improve the business environment, attract more quality investment and ultimately advance sustainable development. The following policy recommendations summarise the key findings from these discussions.

Policy harmonisation can reduce costs, mitigate uncertainty and enhance sustainable business practices for companies in emerging markets. In this context, a whole-of-government approach can ease the complexities of the regulatory environment and ensure consistency throughout the decision-making process. Africa is a case in point: the African Continental Free Trade Area could promote tariff removal and harmonise fiscal regulations, but its implementation needs investment in infrastructure, monitoring mechanisms and partnerships with the private sector. On the other hand, LAC has one of the lowest levels of intraregional trade in the world, with only 13% of its exports staying in the region in 2021.

Sound investment policies and streamlined administrative procedures can boost FDI. Governments should ensure a level playing field between domestic and foreign investment, and address security concerns, where relevant. Legal and regulatory stability can mitigate risk perception and increase FDI in emerging markets. There is a need to promote more collaboration between public and private sectors on policies related to skills development, investment in information and communication technologies, and investment regulations and policies.

Collecting sector-specific data at a granular level can help better estimate the feasibility of projects and their return on investment. In 2023, Africa still encountered difficulty in acquiring high-frequency macro-economic and project-level data, leading to increased due diligence expenses, and further complicating investment evaluations. Data production and sharing between governments and the private sector can inform sound policy measures and foster policy dialogue, to address social and environmental concerns. Amplifying success stories can help support the private sector's perception of the viability of green investment projects.

To promote socially responsible practices, it is important to develop sustainable financial markets, further promote the harmonisation of frameworks and standards for ESG criteria and facilitate access to reliable ESG metrics. Integrating gender equality and diversity and inclusion policies should be a fundamental component of a company's strategy to enhance productivity and innovation.

Encouraging circular business models, leveraging innovative financial tools and adopting key performance indicators to monitor sustainability performance across value chains, are key actions policy makers should prioritise. Improving the implementation of sustainable finance mechanisms can also help accelerate the green transition in emerging markets. Governments can help facilitate private sector adoption of these instruments by ensuring a sound legal framework for investors.

Policy makers should implement sustainability requirements that align with the capacities of small and medium enterprises (SMEs), including designing realistic objectives that can be fully integrated into business operations. SMEs play a central role in emerging economies: in LAC, they represent 99.5% of firms and created 60% of formal productive employment in 2019. Governments and foreign investors should work together to support domestic SMEs' development and encourage the adoption of more green and digital technologies. Facilitating access to finance is imperative to providing support to small-scale farmers, particularly in sub-Saharan Africa.

Public-private dialogue results in more stable investment policy frameworks, more long-term infrastructure investment and sound fiscal policies. Public-private collaboration on innovation, infrastructure and clean technologies can accelerate sustainable economic and social development across emerging and developing economies. Public-private co-investment in innovation, infrastructure and clean energy, like the European Union's Global Gateway Initiative, can foster the green transition in emerging economies.

Companies should further tailor sustainable business models to local contexts, aligning strategies with the needs of local communities and forming partnerships with local suppliers and SMEs. Ongoing green and digital transitions will require innovative policies in workforce reskilling, job creation and support of displaced workers. As much as 10.5% net jobs could be created in LAC by 2030 with a green and just transition.

Central Bank Digital Currencies (CBDCs): What is in it for Emerging Markets?

The 2008-09 Global Financial Crisis challenged the foundations of modern banking. This watershed moment, coupled with rapid advances in financial technology, has led to a proliferation of new financial products and processes in economies around the world. Significant global trends include the end-to-end digital transformation of financial services, the rapid adoption of digital payment products and, more recently, cryptocurrencies and blockchain-enabled products.

Over the past five years, central banks across the world – particularly in emerging markets – have considered or initiated the digitisation of their currencies by introducing some form of Central Bank Digital Currencies (CBDCs). CBDCs could bring disruptive change to the global financial system and facilitate financial inclusion in emerging markets. Many central banks have produced concept notes and launched pilots of CBDCs. It is useful to explore the potential benefits and risks associated with the introduction of CDBCs in developed and emerging economies. Our case studies of the Bahamas, Brazil, the People's Republic of China, India and Nigeria demonstrate the effects related to specific design and implementation processes of CBDCs.

1 Trends in foreign direct investment into emerging markets

This chapter provides an overview of the economic outlook for emerging and developing countries and examines trends in foreign direct investment (FDI) between 2021-23, a period marked by uncertainty and trade disruptions.

Key messages

- In 2023 emerging and developing economies exhibited robust growth rates, with Emerging Asia[1] predicted to experience the highest gross domestic product (GDP) increase in the period 2023-2025.
- Investment patterns worldwide, and particularly foreign direct investment (FDI), weakened in 2023 on the back of tight global financial conditions, higher uncertainty amid intensified geopolitical tensions and the unwinding of pandemic-related fiscal support measures.
- Emerging Asia exhibited contrasting trends in trade in 2023. FDI dropped by 16% for ASEAN and by 6% for the People's Republic of China (hereafter "China"). However, the attractiveness of the region for manufacturing investment remains robust, sustained by the growth in greenfield project announcements, due to competitive wages, increasing domestic demand driven by population growth, and improvements in business regulation and infrastructure.
- In Africa, the potential of FDI to foster sustainable development remains largely untapped, primarily due to the limited integration of FDI into domestic productive activities. In this context, the renewable energy and the service sectors present opportunities for growth. The tertiary sector represented nearly 50% of announced projects between 2021-23 on the continent, thanks to the emergence of new technologies and growing domestic demand.
- Latin America and the Caribbean (LAC) exhibits high FDI inflows, with the region becoming the leading recipient of FDI relative to its gross domestic product (GDP) at 4% in 2021. Prioritising investment in strategic sectors, such as renewable energy and digital transformation, presents a gateway for LAC countries to further promote social and economic development.
- Since 2015, international investment in renewable energy has been experiencing remarkable growth, tripling in magnitude. However, in emerging markets, the high cost of capital and inadequate quality of infrastructure stand as significant barriers to attracting more investment in this sector.
- Special Economic Zones (SEZs) have emerged as pivotal instruments to promote foreign investment, seeking to mitigate costs of doing business and offering attractive incentives. However, data reveal contrasting trends. In LAC, SEZs exhibited a similar average capital influx as the overall region, albeit with slightly lower job intensity. Africa, however, presented a distinct trend, with FDI into SEZs yielding around three times more jobs on average than in the broader region and with average capital expenditure (CAPEX) being nearly four times higher.

Global growth shows resilience amid unexpected international shocks

The global economic landscape is negatively affected by the shocks stemming from persisting high geopolitical risks, coupled with the tightening of monetary policy announced by central banks to counteract rising inflationary pressures (OECD, 2023[1]). Despite a context of uncertainty, OECD analysis shows that global growth has been surprisingly resilient (see Table 1.1). Notably, commodity-producing emerging and developing economies have collectively maintained strong growth rates close to those observed prior to the COVID-19 pandemic (OECD, 2023[1]). GDP growth in Emerging Asia is estimated to have risen to 5.4% in 2023, but is predicted to slow to 5.2% in 2024 and 4.8% in 2025, mainly due to a lower forecast for the People's Republic of China (hereafter "China"). LAC is expected to see its GDP growth rate decline from 2.5% in 2023 to 1.9% in 2024, followed by a rise in 2025 to 2.5%. This forecast reflects the negative growth in Argentina as part of significant policy adjustments to restore macroeconomic stability (IMF, 2024[2]), as well as a normalisation of growth, together with the effects of tighter policies, a weaker external environment and lower commodity prices (IMF, 2023[3]). GDP growth in Sub-Saharan Africa is estimated to have decreased to 3.3% in 2023, but the economy is projected to rebound again to 3.8% and 4.1%, respectively, in the following two years (IMF, 2024[2]). The slowdown reflects adverse weather conditions, global economic uncertainty and domestic supply issues, including electricity (IMF, 2023[3]). Finally, GDP growth in the Middle East and Northern Africa (MENA) is projected to rise from 1.9% in 2023 to 2.7% in 2024 and 4.2% in 2025. In 2024, factors such as the evolving conflicts in the Middle East and Russia's war of aggression against Ukraine, oil production cuts and tight monetary policies have contributed to a return to the low growth of the decade before the global COVID-19 pandemic (OECD, 2024[4]) (IMF, 2024[5]).

Table 1.1. Projections of real GDP growth (in %) for the period 2023-25

Region	2023	2024	2025
Sub-Saharan Africa	3.3	3.8	4.1
Middle East and North Africa	1.9	2.7	4.2
Latin America and the Caribbean	2.5	1.9	2.5
Emerging Asia	5.4	5.2	4.8
India	6.7	6.2	6.5
China (People's Republic of)	5.2	4.7	4.2
OECD	1.7	1.4	1.8
World	3.1	2.9	3.0

Source: (OECD, 2024[6]), *OECD Economic Outlook, Interim Report February 2024: Strengthening the Foundations for Growth*, OECD Publishing, Paris, https://doi.org/10.1787/0fd73462-en, (IMF, 2023[3]), *World Economic Outlook: Navigating Global Divergences*, International Monetary Fund, Washington DC, www.imf.org/en/Publications/WEO/Issues/2023/10/10/world-economic-outlook-october-2023, (World Bank, 2024[7]), *Middle East and North Africa Economic Update: Conflict and Debt in the Middle East and North Africa*, International Bank for Reconstruction and Development/The World Bank, Washington DC, https://www.worldbank.org/en/region/mena/publication/middle-east-and-north-africa-economic-update.

FDI flows into emerging countries rebound after the COVID-19 pandemic

FDI can be a key driver in advancing progress towards the Sustainable Development Goals (SDGs). For host countries, FDI offers opportunities to boost economic growth and innovation, create quality jobs and build human capital, and improve living standards and environmental sustainability. However, while FDI has the potential to contribute significantly to sustainable development, achieving these outcomes depends on aligning the objectives of the private sector with supportive policies from both home and host countries. It is also crucial to continuously monitor and assess the impact of FDI on sustainable development (OECD, 2019[8]).

Restrictions linked to the COVID-19 pandemic negatively affected international trade and cross-border investments due to supply chain disruptions, reduced demand and low business confidence (OECD, 2020[9]). In 2020-21, high-income countries attracted 61% of global greenfield FDI, the highest share ever recorded, compared to 17% for developing Asia, 10% for Latin America and the Caribbean and only 6% for Africa, at the lowest share since 2004 (AUC/OECD, 2023[10]). In 2022, FDI towards emerging economies peaked, with 5 991 projects and USD 632.8 billion invested. However, the momentum slowed in the first six months of 2023, with announced greenfield investment overall showing a stall compared to the second half of 2022 (OECD, 2023[11]). Total announcements of greenfield investment experienced a slight decrease from 4 705 in 2022 to 4 644 in 2023, although the overall CAPEX slightly increased over the same period (see Figure 1.1). Companies investing in emerging markets are predominantly headquartered in advanced economies, primarily in the United States, followed by Germany and the United Kingdom. Between 2020 and 2023, multinational enterprises headquartered in OECD countries initiated around 75% of the new projects announced in emerging and developing economies and created over 3 million new jobs (fDi Markets, 2023[12]).

Figure 1.1. Announced greenfield FDI into emerging markets by destination, 2020-23

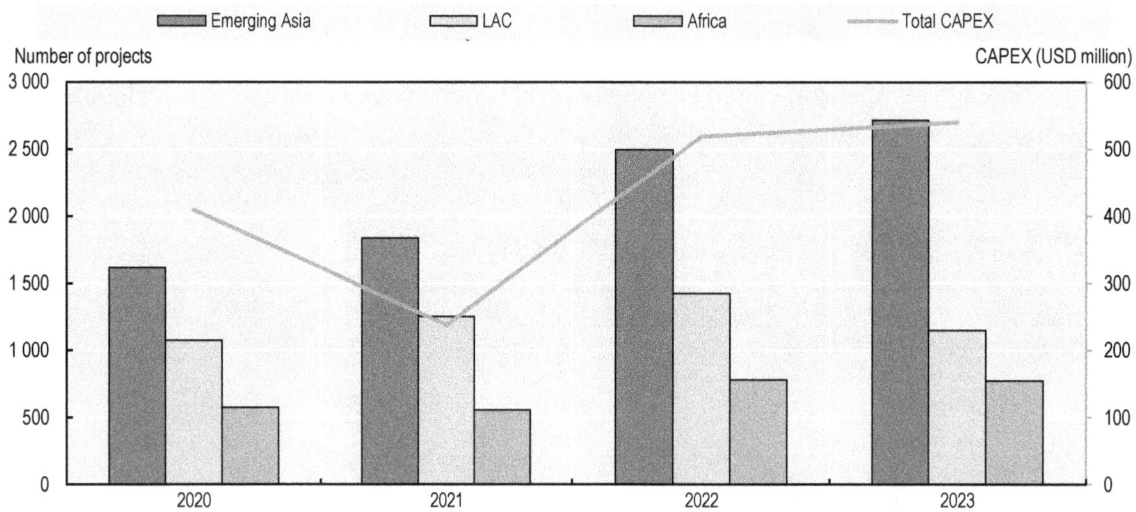

Source: Authors' calculations based on (fDi Markets, 2023[12]), *fDi Markets database*, www.fdimarkets.com (accessed on 17 January 2024).

The LAC region experienced a moderate growth in FDI inflows between 2020-22. Notably, in 2022, Brazil received 41% of the regional total FDI inflows and was ranked as the fifth-largest destination for global FDI (NU.CEPAL, 2023[13]). Mexico attracted 17% of total regional FDI, followed by Chile (9%), Colombia (8%), Argentina (7%), and Peru (5%). Additionally, the region witnessed a significant surge in FDI project announcements, soaring by 93% in 2022 (NU.CEPAL, 2023[13]). However, announced FDI in LAC overall decreased in 2023, with some significant exceptions. Brazil, the largest economy in the region, maintained stable numbers, while Mexico, the second largest economy, saw a 21% increase in greenfield FDI and strengthened its position as the third-top destination for global foreign investments, after India and China (UNCTAD, 2024[14]). In terms of strategic sectors for greenfield FDI, renewable energy has surpassed fossil fuels almost without fail since 2011, particularly in countries such as Chile, the Dominican Republic, Honduras, Paraguay and Uruguay, which emerged as key destinations for FDI in renewable energy over the period 2003-22 (OECD et al., 2023[15]).

Africa's FDI inflows remained nearly unchanged in 2023 compared to the previous year. South Africa, Egypt and Morocco emerged as the top three foreign investment destinations between 2020 and 2023.

Moreover, the region experienced a rise in greenfield FDI project announcements, notably in Kenya, Morocco and Nigeria. However, a one-third reduction in project finance deals has raised concerns for the future of infrastructure financing on the continent (UNCTAD, 2024[14]). In this context, the implementation of the African Continental Free Trade Agreement has the potential to boost FDI in Africa by liberalising trade and harmonising investment regulations (AUC/OECD, 2023[10]).

FDI trends in Emerging Asia are expected to be resilient. India and China, the region's two largest economies, accounted for the highest number of announced FDI projects between 2020 and 2023, capturing 20% and 33%, respectively. Nevertheless, greenfield investment has decreased over the last decade in China, signalling a divergence in investment trends between the country and the rest of the world (FDI Intelligence, 2022[16]). FDI flows to members of the Association of Southeast Asian Nations (ASEAN) declined by 16% in 2023 compared to 2022. However, the region continued to attract manufacturing investments, with a noteworthy increase in greenfield project announcements in countries such as Cambodia, Indonesia, Malaysia, the Philippines, Thailand and Viet Nam, thanks to the increasing liberalisation of the economy and the introduction of effective policies to promote investment (UNCTAD, 2024[14]). Overall, the outlook for FDI is expected to remain resilient in Emerging Asia, as the region attracts investments from a diversified group of countries due to competitive wages, increasing domestic demand driven by population growth, and improvements in business regulations and infrastructure (OECD, 2023[17]).

Special economic zones experience contrasting effects in FDI attraction

Special economic zones (SEZs) have emerged as pivotal instruments in industrial policy, seeking to mitigate the costs of doing business and to offer pockets of stability and efficiency. Their rise in popularity over recent decades is due to their significant role in the broader strategy to attract private investment, particularly FDI (OECD, 2023[18]). However, their effectiveness varies across regions, indicating that successful implementation relies on more than just tax incentives or regulatory simplification. On the other hand, reduced corporate income tax provisions, import duty exemptions and indirect tax abatements may contribute to reducing government revenues, without necessarily providing a benefit to the country concerned (OECD/EUIPO, 2018[19]). In order to be effective, SEZs need to be embedded in a holistic enabling environment, encompassing infrastructure development to integrate SEZs with global and local markets, co-ordinated institutional frameworks, international partnerships, and enhanced environmental, social and governance (ESG) standards (UNCTAD, 2023[20]). Data reveals contrasting trends in job creation and capital investment within SEZs in emerging markets. In Emerging Asia over the period 2021-23, SEZs attracted, on average, lower capital and generated fewer jobs from FDI than the overall region. In LAC, SEZs exhibited a similar average capital influx as the overall region, albeit with slightly lower job intensity. Africa, however, presented a distinct trend, with FDI into SEZs yielding around three times more jobs on average than in the broader region and with average capital expenditure (CAPEX) being nearly four times higher (see Figure 1.2).

Figure 1.2. Average jobs created and CAPEX invested within FDI into SEZs, 2021 23

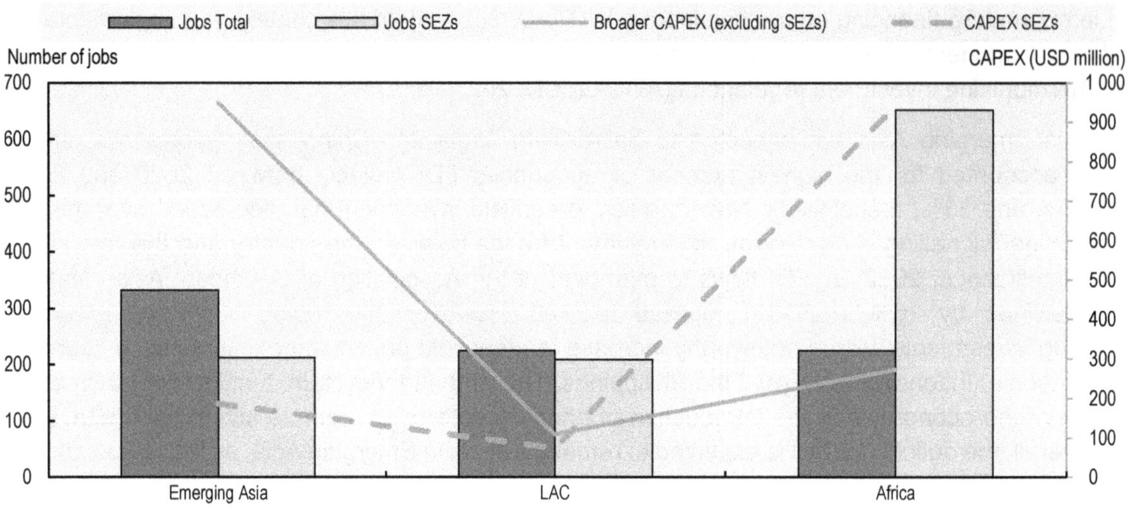

Source: Authors' calculations based on (fDi Markets, 2023[12]), *fDi Markets database*, www.fdimarkets.com (accessed on 17 January 2024).

Despite FDI surges in renewable energy, challenges persist in emerging markets

Since 2015, international investment in renewable energy has experienced remarkable growth, tripling in magnitude (UNCTAD, 2023[21]). By 2017, FDI in renewables was close to 80% of FDI in the primary energy sector for BRICs and over 60% for the OECD. Other regions are quickly gaining ground, notably Southeast Asia and LAC, where FDI flows in renewables grew to over a third and a quarter of FDI in primary energy, respectively (compared to 0% and 5% in 2003) (OECD, 2019[8]) (OECD, 2024[22]). However, despite this upward trajectory, there was a noticeable slowdown in growth in 2022. Furthermore, a significant portion of investment in renewable energy is concentrated in only a few countries, including Brazil, Chile, and India. The solar and wind power sectors stand out, accounting for 95% of these investments (IRENA, 2023[23]). In terms of greenfield investment, renewable energy exhibited a remarkable surge, with both announced capital investment and the number of greenfield projects steadily increasing since 2012 (Knutsson and Ibarlucea Flores, 2022[24]) and surpassing greenfield activity in fossil fuels (see Figure 1.3).

However, despite the promising growth in greenfield investment announcements, international project finance deals, typically larger in scale, have experienced a decline (UNCTAD, 2023[21]). In this context, multinationals can play a critical role in the deployment and innovation of renewable energy technologies across borders. FDI in renewable energy can bolster the economies of emerging markets, but it also represents a considerable chance to progress towards SDGs, which can be assessed through various FDI quality indicators. More investment in renewables can allow emerging economies to turn away from fossil fuels and to reduce their carbon emissions. It is also conducive to creating new jobs, which stimulates employment growth, as well as promotes green, skilled, quality jobs (OECD, 2019[8]). In Africa, developing renewable energy and sustainable infrastructure could generate over 9 million new jobs by 2030 and a further 3 million jobs by 2050 (AUC/OECD, 2024[25]).

Renewable energy has emerged as a significant source of FDI and has indeed been instrumental in job creation globally. In 2022, the renewable energy sector employed 13.7 million people, representing an increase of one million from the previous year. Asia hosts around 66% of these jobs, with China alone contributing 41% of the global total (IRENA and ILO, 2023[26]). In emerging economies, the high cost of initial capital investment stands as a significant barrier to attracting investment in renewable energies. Additionally, inadequate infrastructure, particularly concerning energy storage and grid integration, together with the lack of readiness of distribution infrastructures, pose a significant hindrance to the widespread adoption of renewable energy sources (IRENA, 2023[23]).

Figure 1.3. Energy greenfield FDI into emerging markets, 2003-23

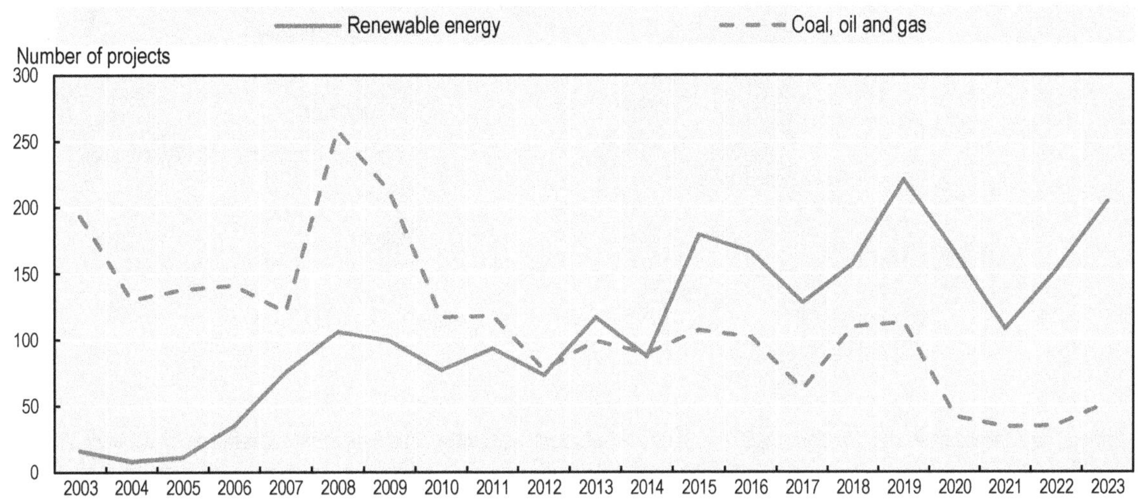

Note: Emerging markets include Africa, LAC and Emerging Asia.
Source: Authors' calculations based on (fDi Markets, 2023[12]), *fDi Markets database*, www.fdimarkets.com (accessed on 17 January 2024).

Africa sees growing FDI inflows for tertiary and renewable energy sectors

The potential of FDI to contribute to sustainable growth in Africa remains largely untapped. This is primarily due to its limited integration with productive activities on the continent. Enhancing FDI in Africa holds the potential to stimulate growth, foster innovation, and enhance human capital through spillovers to local suppliers and domestically owned enterprises (AUC/OECD, 2023[10]). Notably, intra-African greenfield FDI demonstrates greater resilience to global shocks compared to FDI originating from outside the continent. In the period 2020-21, intra-African greenfield FDI witnessed a decrease of 20% from its 2018-19 levels, whereas FDI from outside the continent experienced a substantially steeper drop of 58% (AUC/OECD, 2023[10]). Between 2021 and 2023, South African and Nigerian companies emerged as the most dynamic players in the intra-African market, while, in the same period, the United States, the United Kingdom, France and the United Arab Emirates stood out as the main source markets for foreign companies investing in Africa.

In recent years, the emergence of new technologies and growing domestic demand led to an increase in FDI in the tertiary sector, which represented nearly 50% of announced projects between 2021-23 on the continent (AUC/OECD, 2023[10]). This included investments in business services, as well as in sales, marketing and support. Additionally, manufacturing continued to hold significant importance, representing 17% of announced projects in the period (see Figure 1.4).

Figure 1.4. Announced greenfield FDI in Africa by business activities, 2021-23

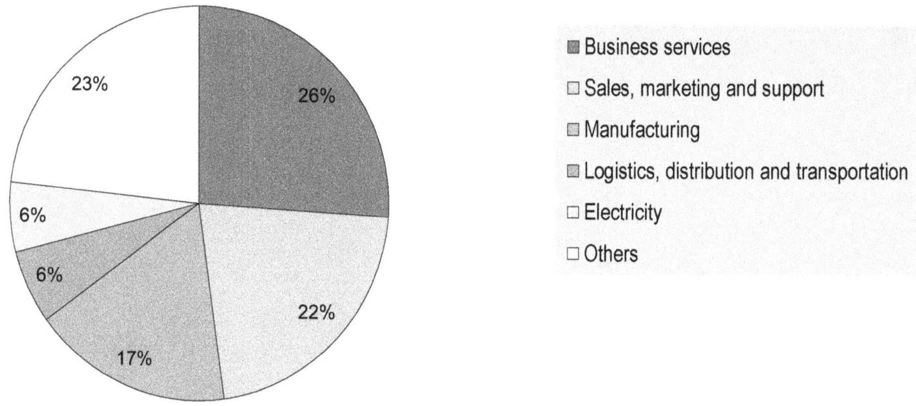

Source: Authors' calculations based on (fDi Markets, 2023[12]), *fDi Markets database*, www.fdimarkets.com (accessed on 17 January 2024).

The potential of FDI to foster sustainable development remains underexploited. For example, while it has been estimated that USD 1 million in FDI creates 14 jobs in textiles, 10 in electronic equipment and 9 in automotive, these sectors attracted only 4.5% of greenfield FDI to African countries over the period 2003-20 (AUC/OECD, 2023[10]). Therefore, the capacity of FDI to stimulate employment on the continent remains limited. Conversely, Africa received a considerable inflow of renewable energy projects, accompanied by substantial capital investment totalling over USD 200 billion, underscoring the continent's potential to become a global green powerhouse (see Figure 1.5). At present, hydropower is the largest source of renewable electricity in Africa, particularly in Angola, the Democratic Republic of the Congo (hereafter "DRC"), Egypt, Ethiopia, Ghana, Morocco, Mozambique, Nigeria, South Africa, Sudan and Zambia (IRENA/AfDB, 2022[27]). Among the most recently announced projects is the USD 37 billion green hydrogen project planned near the north-east of Nouakchott, Mauritania. Its construction was announced by Infinity Power, a joint venture company of Egypt-based Infinity and United Arab Emirates-based Masdar, after signing a memorandum of understanding with Germany-based Conjuncta and the government of Mauritania in March 2023 (Reuters, 2023[28]).

Figure 1.5. Announced greenfield FDI in Africa by sector (top 10), 2021-23

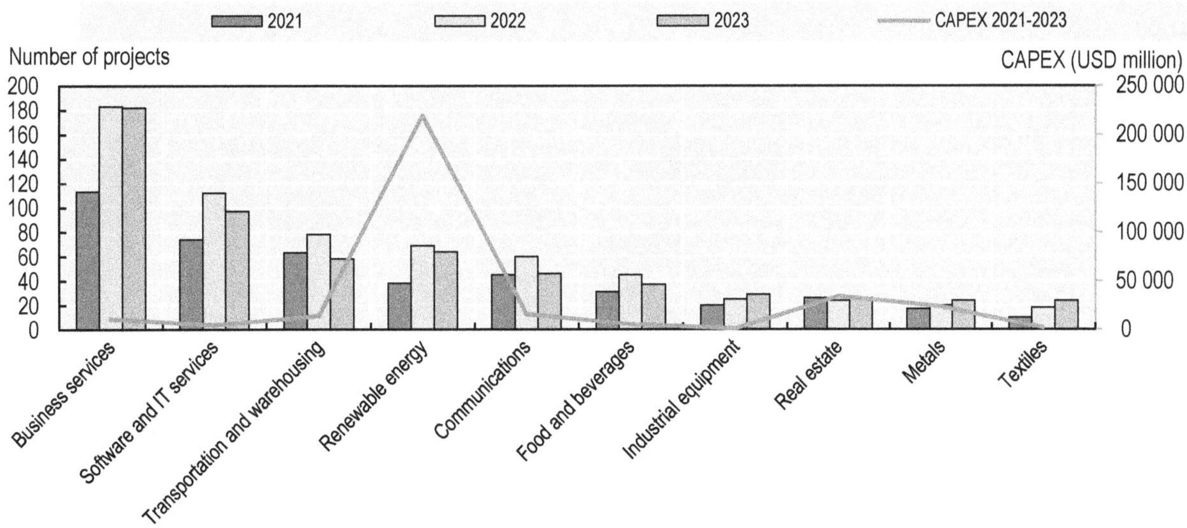

Source: Authors' calculations based on (fDi Markets, 2023[12]), *fDi Markets database*, www.fdimarkets.com (accessed on 17 January 2024).

FDI into the technology and renewable energy sectors has the potential to accelerate economic development in LAC

The total investment trajectory for LAC has exhibited a general deceleration over the past three decades. While investment levels vary across countries, the overall trend has been lagging compared to other regions, with total investment averaging 20.4% of GDP by 2022 compared to 40% in Emerging Asia (OECD et al., 2023[15]). Despite low domestic investment, the region has attracted relatively high levels of FDI. In 2022 alone, LAC received USD 112 billion in FDI, signifying a substantial 60% increase from 2021 and becoming the first world region to attract FDI inflows of 4% relative to its GDP, while Asia-Pacific held the second position at 2% (OECD et al., 2023[15]). FDI had a significant impact on job creation in the region, accounting for 898 855 new jobs in the period 2021-23. The distribution of these jobs varies significantly depending on the country of origin and the sector receiving the investment. Notably, FDI in renewables created more jobs than in fossil fuels, demonstrating the potential of green investment to stimulate employment in the LAC region (OECD et al., 2023[15]). In 2022, the share of intra-regional greenfield project announcements remained relatively small, at 11% of all projects in the region (8% in terms of value), although showing an increase since 2017, when it was 8% of the total (6% in value) (UNCTAD, 2023[21]). Argentinian and Mexican companies emerged as the two main investors in intra-regional FDI with 97 and 90 announced projects and a CAPEX of USD 4.8 billion and USD 3.4 billion, respectively, between 2021-23 (fDi Markets, 2023[12]). The United States, followed by Germany, Spain, the United Kingdom and China, emerged as the main source markets for FDI in LAC over the same period. Investment allocation across value-chain activities exhibits considerable diversity. Between 2021-23, manufacturing represented nearly a quarter of greenfield FDI (23%). Business services and sales, marketing and support each accounted for 18% of total projects in the period (see Figure 1.6).

Figure 1.6. Announced greenfield FDI in LAC by business activities, 2021-23

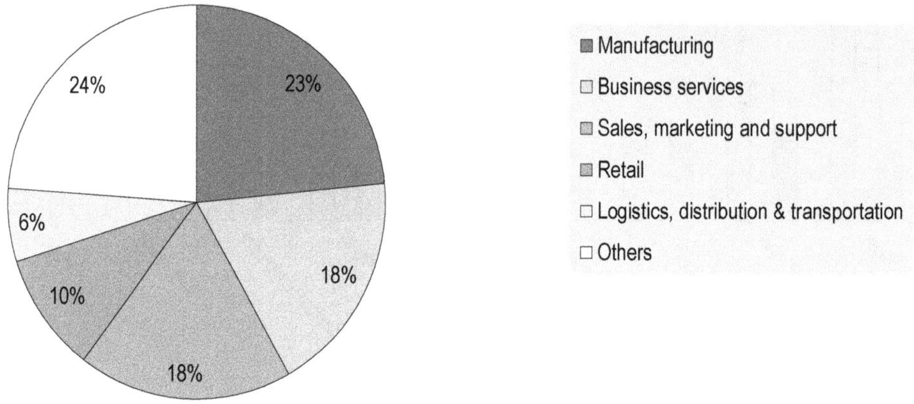

Source: Authors' calculations based on (fDi Markets, 2023[12]), fDi Markets database, www.fdimarkets.com (accessed on 22 October 2024).

Projects in renewable energy exhibited considerably high CAPEX despite being concentrated in a lower number of projects compared to other sectors (see Figure 1.7). Recent analyses show that prioritising investment in strategic sectors, such as technology and renewable energy, presents a gateway for LAC countries to capitalise on untapped opportunities, particularly in the realms of green transition and digital transformation (OECD et al., 2023[15]). LAC already has one of the cleanest electricity sectors in the world as renewables, led by hydropower, generated 60% of the region's electricity in 2023, twice the global average, and countries such as Argentina, Brazil, Chile and Mexico stood out as solar and wind energy powerhouses (IEA, 2023[29]). In this context, the transition towards green energy represents an opportunity for the region's productive evolution, underscoring the need for countries to prioritise green energy projects within their productive development strategies and agendas to realise the region's untapped potential in terms of natural resources (NU.CEPAL, 2023[13]).

The automotive industry also holds significant importance in LAC, as it boasts extensive linkages with other industries and enjoys favourable conditions for producing electric mobility components (OECD et al., 2021[30]). For example, in 2023, US-based electric vehicle manufacturer Tesla Motors announced plans to open a new electric vehicle manufacturing facility in Monterrey, Mexico. With a commitment exceeding USD 5 billion, the company aims to generate approximately 7 000 jobs (Reuters, 2023[31]).

Figure 1.7. Announced greenfield FDI in LAC by sector (top 10), 2021-23

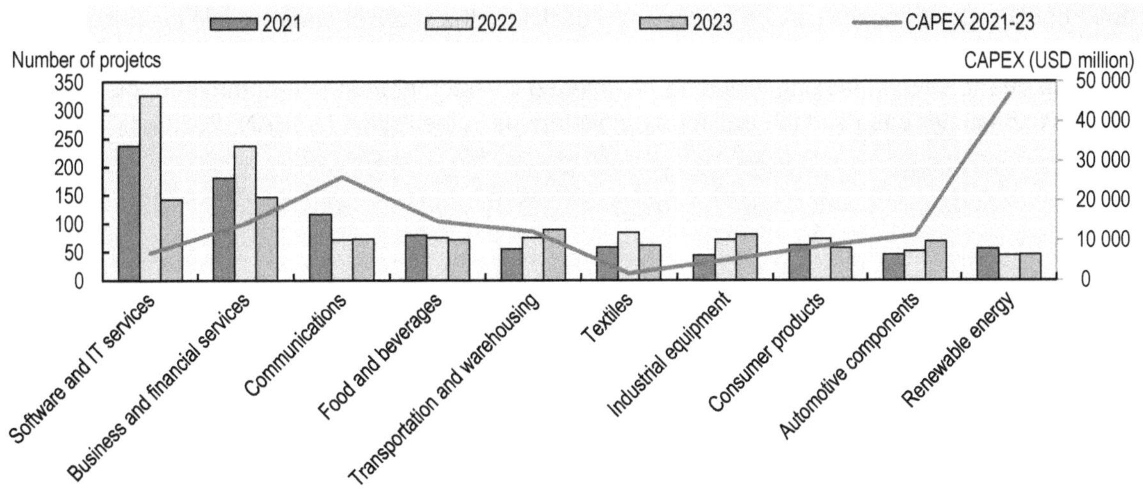

Source: Authors' calculations based on (fDi Markets, 2023[12]), *fDi Markets database*, www.fdimarkets.com (accessed on 17 January 2024).

ASEAN strengthens its position as an important regional destination for FDI

In 2023, FDI announcements into Emerging Asia slightly increased compared to 2022, with some major economies, such as China and India, seeing a relative decline. However, total CAPEX on greenfield investment in the region has strongly increased since 2022 (see Figure 1.8).

Figure 1.8. Announced greenfield FDI in Emerging Asia, 2020 23

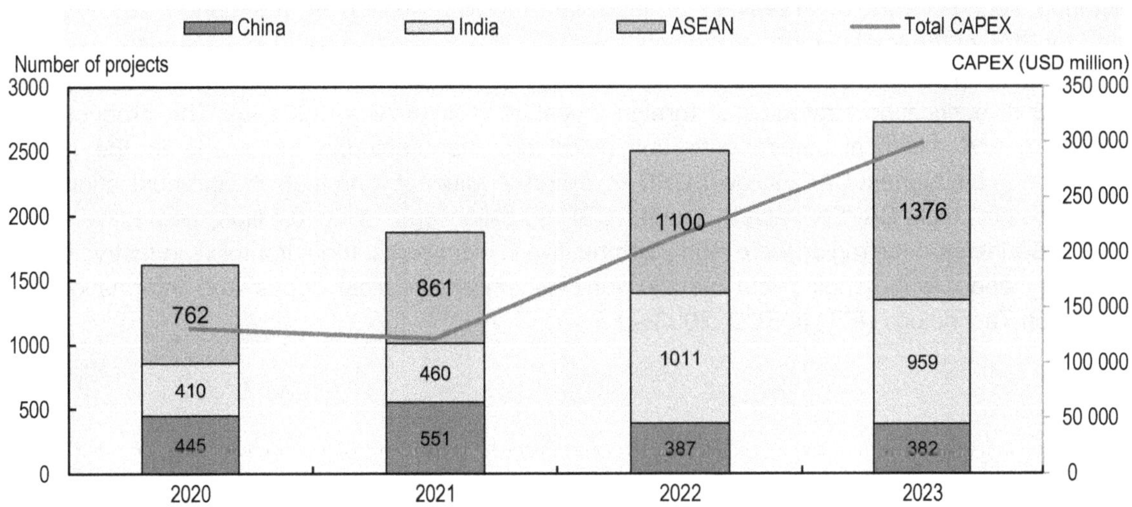

Source: Authors' calculations based on (fDi Markets, 2023[12]), *fDi Markets database*, www.fdimarkets.com (accessed on 17 January 2024).

Emerging Asia, an engine of FDI growth, experienced declines in 2023. FDI dropped by 16% for ASEAN and by 6% for China (OECD, 2024[32]). Tighter global credit conditions contributed to the temporary slowdown in FDI in 2022 and 2023, yet signs of recovery are already visible (OECD, 2023[17]). The region is predicted to remain attractive for FDI due to competitive wages, increasing domestic demand driven by population growth, and improvements in business regulations and infrastructure (OECD, 2023[17]). Nearly half of all announced FDI projects between 2021-23 were concentrated in sales, marketing and support (26%), and business services (25%) (see Figure 1.9). Since 2010, there has been an increase in the share of FDI inflows into the service sector and a decline in the share channelled into the primary sector (industries involved in the extraction and production of raw materials) in these economies (OECD, 2023[17]). This trend is due to several factors, including heightened investor interest in e-commerce, the rise of the middle-class consumer base and the proliferation of startups in the region (ASEAN, 2023[33]).

Figure 1.9. Announced greenfield FDI in Emerging Asia by business activities, 2021-23

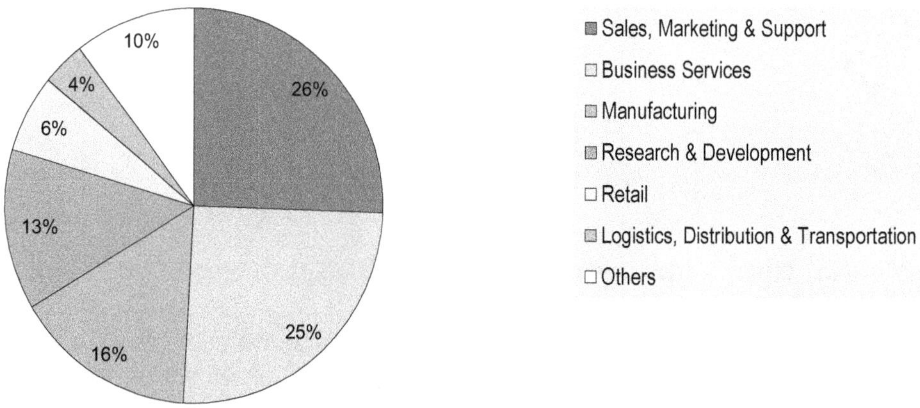

Source: Authors' calculations based on (fDi Markets, 2023[12]), *fDi Markets database*, www.fdimarkets.com (accessed on 17 January 2024).

Manufacturing secured 16% of greenfield projects in Emerging Asia over the period 2021-23 and accounted for 25% of the total number of projects in China. This increasing trend in investment attraction signifies the changing patterns in FDI destination in Emerging Asia, with ASEAN countries benefiting from de-risking and diversification strategies of foreign investors (Nikkei Asia, 2024[34]). The production of semiconductors and electrical components dominated the manufacturing landscape in the region, presenting among the highest CAPEX, over USD 60 billion. Additionally, projects in communications and real estate boasted high CAPEX values, around USD 50 billion and USD 40 billion, respectively (see Figure 1.10). Countries in the region were highly competitive in electronics, the automotive industry, textiles and machinery and are expanding into electric vehicles, pharmaceutical goods and Information and Communication Technology (ICT) (OECD, 2023[35]).

Figure 1.10. Announced greenfield FDI in Asia by sector (top 10), 2021-23

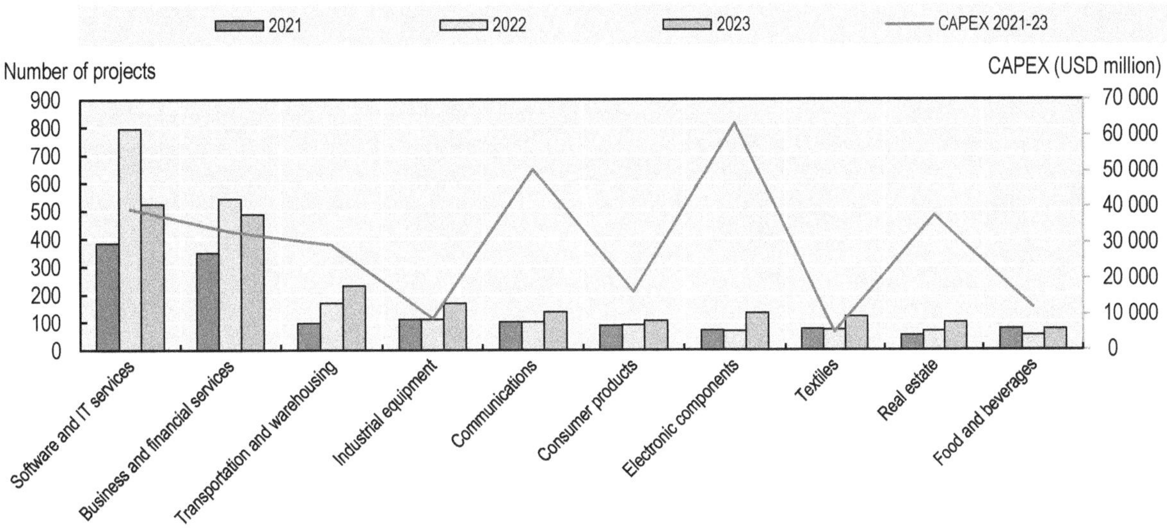

Source: Authors' calculations based on (fDi Markets, 2023[12]), *fDi Markets database*, www.fdimarkets.com (accessed on 17 January 2024).

In the period 2021-23, India retained its position among the top five recipients of global greenfield projects, with a quarter of these projects dedicated to research and development (see Figure 1.11). Noteworthy projects include a USD 5 billion investment for urea production from green hydrogen in a joint venture between the Adani Group and TotalEnergies, as well as the construction of one of India's first semiconductor chip factories by Foxconn and Vedanta Resources for USD 19 billion (UNCTAD, 2023[20]). The Indian government has included in the 2023-24 budget a large sum to fund improvements in infrastructure and connectivity, which, coupled with strong demographic growth, is projected to increase FDI inflows into manufacturing in the long term (OECD, 2023[35]). The 2024-2025 India Union budget envisages sustained support to 9 priorities, including manufacturing and services, infrastructure, and energy security (Ministry of Finance, 2024[36]).

In China, the decline in greenfield projects can be attributed to several factors, including rising labour costs, the need for firms to diversify their supply chains, and the transition towards a more service-oriented economy. This trend was further accelerated by the COVID-19 pandemic (FDI Intelligence, 2022[16]). However, China remains the world's second-largest recipient of FDI in 2023, with a 5% increase from 2022, with investment concentrated in manufacturing and high-tech industries, largely driven by European Multinational Enterprises (MNEs) (UNCTAD, 2023[20]). ASEAN surpassed China as a recipient of FDI in 2021 for the first time (ASEAN, 2023[33]). Robust growth in manufacturing, energy transition investments (including renewables and electric mobility), retail trade and the digital economy were all key in the development of ASEAN countries (ASEAN, 2023[33]). Notably, Singapore accounted for 60% of the region's total investments, while Malaysia, Singapore and Viet Nam achieved record FDI levels in 2023 (ASEAN, 2023[33]). Additionally, Cambodia has emerged as a prominent FDI recipient among lesser-developed countries (UNCTAD, 2023[20]). Despite ASEAN's importance as an FDI destination, only 20% of these investments are intraregional, compared with 60% in the European Union (ASEAN, 2023[33]). Nonetheless, the rising middle class is expected to increase the region's world share of demand for consumer goods (OECD, 2023[17]). Some economies in the region, such as Indonesia, Malaysia and Thailand, among others, lack export diversification and, therefore, are highly vulnerable to commodity price changes, including energy pricing and changes in global demand and supply (OECD, 2023[35]). Factors such as economic liberalisation and policies aimed at promoting FDI have played pivotal roles in attracting investments from major sources such as the United States, Europe and China, which are the largest sources of FDI inflows in these countries (ASEAN, 2023[33]).

Figure 1.11. Announced greenfield FDI in Emerging Asia by region and country as a percentage of business activities, 2021-23

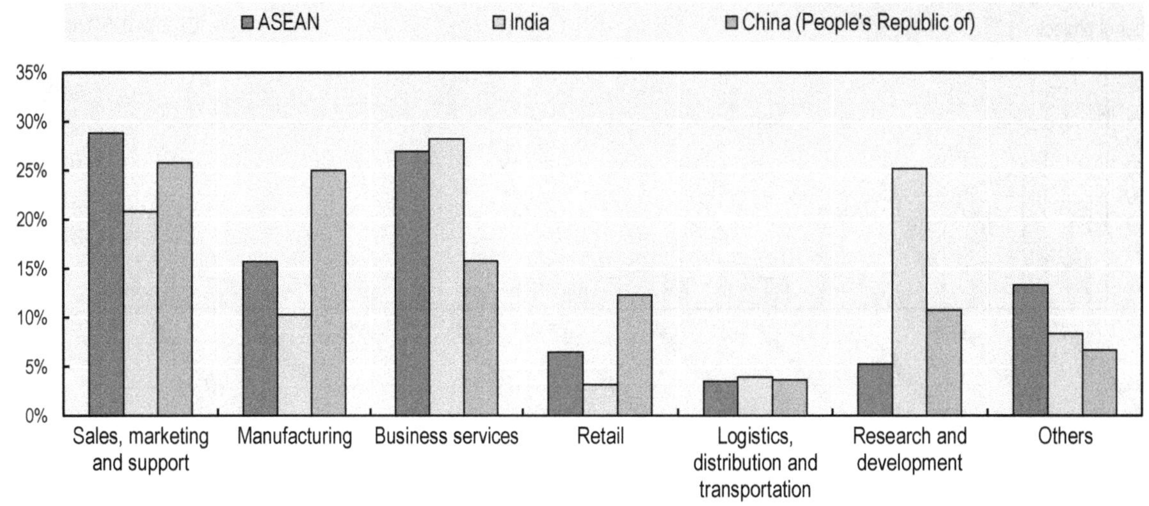

Source: Authors' calculations based on (fDi Markets, 2023[12]), *fDi Markets database*, www.fdimarkets.com (accessed on 17 January 2024).

References

ASEAN (2023), *ASEAN Investment Report 2023 - International Investment Trends Key issues and policy options*, https://asean.org/wp-content/uploads/2023/12/AIR-Special-2023.pdf. [33]

AUC/OECD (2024), *Africa's Development Dynamics 2024: Skills, Jobs and Productivity*, African Union Commission, Addis Ababa/OECD Publishing, Paris, https://doi.org/10.1787/df06c7a4-en. [25]

AUC/OECD (2023), *Africa's Development Dynamics 2023: Investing in Sustainable Development*, African Union Commission, Addis Ababa/OECD Publishing, Paris, https://doi.org/10.1787/3269532b-en. [10]

FDI Intelligence (2022), *China's Foreign Investment Problem*, http://www.fdiintelligence.com/content/locations/global/asia-pacific/china/china-s-foreign-investment-problem-80679 (accessed on 12 February 2024). [16]

fDi Markets (2023), *fDi Markets database*, http://fdimarkets.com (accessed on 17 January 2024). [12]

IEA (2023), *World Energy Outlook 2023*, OECD Publishing, Paris, https://doi.org/10.1787/827374a6-en. [29]

IMF (2024), *Regional Economic Outlook: Middle East and Central Asia*, International Monetary Fund, Washington DC, https://www.imf.org/en/Publications/REO/MECA/Issues/2024/04/18/regional-economic-outlook-middle-east-central-asia-april-2024. [5]

IMF (2024), *World Economic Outlook Uptade: Moderating Inflation and Steady Growth Open Path to Soft Landing*, International Monetary Fund, Washington DC, https://www.imf.org/en/Publications/WEO/Issues/2024/01/30/world-economic-outlook-update-january-2024. [2]

IMF (2023), *World Economic Outlook: Navigating Global Divergences*, International Monetary Fund, Washington DC, http://www.imf.org/en/Publications/WEO/Issues/2023/10/10/world-economic-outlook-october-2023. [3]

IRENA (2023), *World Energy Transitions Outlook 2023: 1.5°C Pathway*, International Renewable Energy Agency, Abu Dhabi., https://mc-cd8320d4-36a1-40ac-83cc-3389-cdn-endpoint.azureedge.net/-/media/Files/IRENA/Agency/Publication/2023/Jun/IRENA_World_energy_transitions_outlook_2023.pdf?rev=db3ca01ecb4a4ef8accb31d017934e97. [23]

IRENA and ILO (2023), *Renewable energy and jobs: Annual review 2023*, International Renewable Energy Agency, Abu Dhabi and International Labour Organization, Geneva, https://mc-cd8320d4-36a1-40ac-83cc-3389-cdn-endpoint.azureedge.net/-/media/Files/IRENA/Agency/Publication/2023/Sep/IRENA_Renewable_energy_and_jobs_2023.pdf?rev=4c35bf5a1222429e8f0bf932a641f818. [26]

IRENA/AfDB (2022), *Renewable Energy Market Analysis: Africa and Its Regions*, International Renewable Energy Agency and African Development Bank, Abu Dhabi and Abidjan, https://www.irena.org/-/media/Files/IRENA/Agency/Publication/2022/Jan/IRENA_Market_Africa_2022.pdf?rev=bb73e285a0974bc996a1f942635ca556. [27]

Knutsson, P. and P. Ibarlucea Flores (2022), "Trends, investor types and drivers of renewable energy FDI", *OECD Working Papers on International Investment*, No. 2022/02, OECD Publishing, Paris, https://doi.org/10.1787/4390289d-en. [24]

Ministry of Finance (2024), *Summary of the Union Budget 2024-2025*, https://www.pib.gov.in/PressReleasePage.aspx?PRID=2035618 (accessed on 27 September 2024). [36]

Nikkei Asia (2024), *India is well placed to become the "next China" and drive global growth*, http://www.asia.nikkei.com/Opinion/India-is-well-placed-to-become-the-next-China-and-drive-global-growth (accessed on 26 September 2024). [34]

NU.CEPAL (ed.) (2023), *Foreign Direct Investment in Latin America and the Caribbean 2023*, ECLAC, Santiago, https://repositorio.cepal.org/items/57c40f34-af3c-4b2f-ab55-71cffe554cfe. [13]

OECD (2024), *2024 Ministerial Council Meeting Statement: co-creating the flow of change: leading global discussions with objective and reliable approaches towards sustainable and inclusive growth.* [4]

OECD (2024), *Economic Outlook for Southeast Asia, China and India 2024: Developing amid Disaster Risks*, OECD Publishing, Paris, https://doi.org/10.1787/3bbe7dfe-en. [32]

OECD (2024), *OECD Economic Outlook, Interim Report February 2024: Strenghtening the Foundations for Growth*, OECD Publishing, Paris, https://doi.org/10.1787/0fd73462-en. [6]

OECD (2024), *Towards More Sustainable Investment Frameworks: Evaluating the Feasibility of Sustainable Investment Facilitation Agreements with Southern Neighbourhood Countries*, OECD Publishing, Paris, https://doi.org/10.1787/411468b9-en. [22]

OECD (2023), "Best practices in investment promotion: An overview of regional state aid and special economic zones in Europe", *OECD Business and Finance Policy Papers*, No. 27, OECD Publishing, Paris, https://doi.org/10.1787/0c8e6ca3-en. [18]

OECD (2023), *Economic Outlook for Southeast Asia, China and India 2023 - Update: Resilience Under Uncertainty*, OECD Publishing, Paris, https://doi.org/10.1787/cd94bcf6-en. [35]

OECD (2023), *Economic Outlook for Southeast Asia, China and India 2023: Reviving Tourism Post-Pandemic*, OECD Publishing, Paris, https://doi.org/10.1787/f677c529-en. [17]

OECD (2023), *Investment in figures*, https://www.oecd.org/investment/statistics.htm (accessed on 6 June 2024). [11]

OECD (2023), *OECD Economic Outlook, Volume 2023 Issue 2*, OECD Publishing, Paris, https://doi.org/10.1787/7a5f73ce-en. [1]

OECD (2020), "OECD investment policy responses to COVID-19", *OECD Policy Responses to Coronavirus (COVID-19)*, OECD Publishing, Paris, https://doi.org/10.1787/4be0254d-en. [9]

OECD (2019), *FDI Qualities Indicators: Measuring the sustainable development impacts of investment*, OECD Publishing, Paris, https://doi.org/10.1787/0894dfba-en. [8]

OECD et al. (2023), *Latin American Economic Outlook 2023: Investing in Sustainable Development*, OECD Publishing, Paris, https://doi.org/10.1787/8c93ff6e-en. [15]

OECD et al. (2021), *Latin American Economic Outlook 2021: Working Together for a Better Recovery*, OECD Publishing, Paris, https://doi.org/10.1787/5fedabe5-en. [30]

OECD/EUIPO (2018), *Trade in Counterfeit Goods and Free Trade Zones: Evidence from Recent Trends*, Illicit Trade, OECD Publishing, Paris/European Union Intellectual Property Office, Alicante, https://doi.org/10.1787/9789264289550-en. [19]

Reuters (2023), *Consortium signs $34 billion MoU for hydrogen project in Mauritania*, https://www.reuters.com/business/energy/german-uae-egypt-consortium-sign-34-bln-deal-hydrogen-project-mauritania-faz-2023-03-08/#:~:text=BERLIN%2C%20March%208%20(Reuters),in%20the%20West%20African%20country. (accessed on 6 February 2024). [28]

Reuters (2023), *Tesla plans gigafactory in first Mexico investment*, https://www.reuters.com/business/autos-transportation/teslas-new-mexico-plant-could-create-up-6000-jobs-foreign-ministry-official-2023-03-01/ (accessed on 14 February 2024). [31]

UNCTAD (2024), *Foreign direct investment in developing economies fell 9% in 2023*, https://unctad.org/news/foreign-direct-investment-developing-economies-fell-9-2023#:~:text=Foreign%20direct%20investment%20(FDI)%20flows,Monitor%2C%20published%20on%2017%20January. (accessed on 5 February 2024). [14]

UNCTAD (2023), *Handbook on Special Economic Zones in Africa*, United Nations Conference on Trade and Development, https://unctad.org/system/files/official-document/diaeia2021d3-overview_en.pdf. [20]

UNCTAD (2023), *World Investment Report*, https://unctad.org/system/files/official-document/wir2023_en.pdf. [21]

World Bank (2024), *Middle East and North Africa Economic Update: Conflict and Debt in the Middle East and North Africa*, International Bank for Reconstruction and Development / The World Bank, Washington DC, https://www.worldbank.org/en/region/mena/publication/middle-east-and-north-africa-economic-update. [7]

Note

[1] In this report, Emerging Asia encompasses the People's Republic of China, India and the ten ASEAN member states: Brunei Darussalam, Cambodia, Indonesia, Lao People's Democratic Republic (hereafter "Lao PDR"), Malaysia, Myanmar, the Philippines, Singapore, Thailand and Viet Nam. ASEAN-5 includes Indonesia, Malaysia, the Philippines, Singapore and Thailand.

2 Private sector insights on emerging markets

This chapter provides insights from the private sector on navigating risks in emerging markets and accelerating sustainable investment in times of uncertainty. The analysis builds on the discussion hosted by the OECD Development Centre's Emerging Markets Network (EMnet) during in-person and virtual meetings in 2023, featuring the participation of high-level policy makers, senior business executives and OECD experts. Further insights originate from desk research and bilateral conversations with EMnet members and multinational companies operating in emerging markets.

Key messages

- EMnet members and partners acknowledged that fostering the stability of regulatory frameworks, streamlining permits and licensing, and enhancing public governance is essential to creating a sound environment for business in emerging markets. Fostering fair competition through modernised regulations, a fair level playing field, and simplified administrative procedures can attract long-term private investment and contribute to sustainable economic development.
- Financial market infrastructure needs to be improved by diversifying the investor base, reinforcing investment protection instruments, and advocating for common green taxonomies across regions.
- EMnet members recognised that international investors are refining their knowledge of emerging markets by adopting a more granular approach in evaluating individual projects and country profiles. More consolidated green taxonomy frameworks have the potential to reduce transaction costs for investors, making capital markets in emerging regions more attractive. There is a challenge in aligning local taxonomies with broader frameworks, and EMnet companies emphasised the need for commonalities to facilitate cross-border investment while addressing local specificities.
- EMnet members and participants considered that regional integration efforts like the African Continental Free Trade Area could catalyse tariff removal and the harmonisation of fiscal regulation. On the other hand, Latin America and the Caribbean (LAC) still presents one of the lowest levels of intraregional trade worldwide, at only 13% in 2021.
- In 2023, emerging countries still encounter difficulty in collecting high-frequency macro-economic and project-level data, which often leads to increased due diligence expenses, and further complicates investment evaluations.
- EMnet members and partners emphasised the need to enhance risk intelligence and data production, as well as to establish sound channels for information sharing between public and private actors, in order to boost investor confidence and strengthen investment in emerging markets.
- EMnet members and partners emphasised the need to integrate gender equality and diversity and inclusion policies, when operating in emerging markets and regard it as a fundamental component of a company's medium- and long-term strategy to enhance productivity and innovation.
- EMnet members and partners stressed the importance of incentivising circular business models, adopting innovative financial tools and implementing key performance indicators to monitor sustainability performance across value chains.
- Further implementing sustainable finance mechanisms, such as green, social, sustainable and sustainability-linked (GSSS) bonds, can help accelerate the green transition in emerging markets. To better manage the financial impact of disasters, it is also important for governments to consider new options, such as catastrophe bonds, insurance pools and disaster risk financing mechanisms.
- It is essential to design sustainability requirements that align with the capacities of micro, small and medium-sized enterprises (MSMEs), as well as to enhance market linkages between MSMEs and multinational enterprises (MNEs), and increase financial support directed to them. As much as 75% of the financing needs of MSMEs in LAC remain unfunded. Promoting tailored policies to enhance green, digital and social transformations, stimulating public-private

collaboration and enabling access to finance are key instruments to support MSMEs in key sectors such as agribusiness.

- Taking inspiration from initiatives like the European Union's Global Gateway, public-private co-investment in innovation, infrastructure and clean energy will be an essential component of the green transition in emerging and developing economies to align investment with effective public policy objectives.
- The private sector can support local communities by tailoring sustainable business models, promoting partnerships with local stakeholders and addressing social issues, such as the reskilling of workers and the promotion of diversity and inclusion.

Reform policies and regulations to enhance a favourable environment for investment

Harmonise policies and enhance regional integration efforts

EMnet members and partners acknowledged that harmonised policies and regulations can facilitate a level playing field by ensuring consistent standards and guidelines for sustainable business conduct. This consistency contributes to reducing uncertainty and compliance costs for companies operating in different markets. By aligning regulations, countries can enhance the transparency and predictability of sustainability requirements, fostering a conducive environment for more sustainable trade and investment. Furthermore, EMnet members and partners emphasised that harmonised policies could incentivise sustainable practices by establishing clear expectations, providing a supportive regulatory framework and facilitating co-operation with public entities and other stakeholders. EMnet members and partners also highlighted the importance of public standardised reporting, which can promote accountability and transparency, enable informed decision making for investors and help build public trust. Advocating for common taxonomies in emerging markets is also important, as it can help increase harmonisation and transparency. In this context, it is necessary to harmonise investment policies and encourage the development of regional production networks. Regional co-operation, policy harmonisation and modernisation are also necessary to ensure economic development in emerging regions. In the case of Africa, the creation of the African Continental Free Trade Area can act as a catalyst for tariff removal and the harmonisation of fiscal regulations between African countries, stimulating intra-African trade and bolstering investor confidence. On the other hand, the Latin America and the Caribbean (LAC) region has one of the lowest levels of intraregional trade in the world, with only 13% of its exports staying in the region in 2021 (OECD et al., 2021[1]). In this context, EMnet members and partners underscored that Latin American governments need to work together to harmonise and co-ordinate investment policies, expanding partnerships with international organisations and development finance institutions to align green norms and regulations and manage the impact of policies adopted in partner countries.

Align national strategies with climate goals

EMnet members and partners highlighted the crucial role of governments in aligning their national strategies with the aspiration of pursuing economic development alongside climate goals. Facilitating green investment such as this also requires enabling conditions and suitable regulatory frameworks. EMnet members and partners advocated for a paradigm shift, recognising emerging regions not just as climate-affected areas but also as potential global green powerhouses. EMnet members and partners identified barriers obstructing green infrastructure investment across regions, primarily rooted in insufficient financial assurances, which are crucial for attracting external capital from private investors. In addressing this, EMnet members and partners emphasised the importance of leveraging established best practices, citing, for example, Kenya's issuance of the Energy Sector White Paper. While not a regulation in itself, the document serves a crucial role in articulating the national strategy and mobilising unified government support (Ministry of Energy, 2022[2]). Without a comprehensive whole-of-government approach, valuable initiatives risk getting entangled in bureaucratic complexities across various government departments, hindering their efficacy and impact. EMnet members and partners underlined that inducing behavioural change in the private sector is not only feasible but essential and that this needs to be supported by public policies through incentives, sound fiscal policies and investment guarantees. Governments can actively support the green transition by promoting innovative blended financial mechanisms, incorporating incentives, and gradually phasing out fossil fuel subsidies. Finally, the success of the green transition in emerging and developing countries depends on the capacity of their governments to decarbonise regional, urban and rural industries through suitable economic, fiscal and financial incentives.

Streamline regulations and create a level playing field for all actors

EMnet members and partners stressed the need for regulatory updates and streamlined administrative procedures to bolster foreign investment. In the case of the digital sector, these needs coincide with the various challenges that digital infrastructure deployment encounters in any country, which, in some cases, are exacerbated in emerging markets. Some of the barriers to the deployment of digital infrastructure are related to the nature of the market structure itself (monopolies or duopolies) with significant barriers to entry, high capital expenditure, geographical considerations, administrative barriers, access to spectrum, regulatory uncertainty, the varying capacity of clients to afford services and devices in emerging markets and, in some instances, a lack of basic infrastructure, such as electricity. Furthermore, EMnet members and partners stressed the importance of governmental bodies, agencies, and both public and private stakeholders establishing a level playing field to avoid discrimination between foreign and domestic direct investments. EMnet members and partners stressed the importance of fostering a secure investment landscape by encouraging fair competition and breaking down existing monopolies. Recognising the need to protect existing investments from value erosion, EMnet members and partners also highlighted the necessity to mitigate volatility and enhance access to foreign exchange markets when securing loans. Furthermore, governments ought to address security concerns facing companies operating within their domestic markets by actively combatting risks associated with terrorism and sabotage.

Foster regulatory stability to mitigate risk perception

The prevailing high-risk perception associated with legal and regulatory instability poses a hindrance to securing finance from shareholders for sustained investment in emerging markets. In this context, it becomes crucial to cultivate a favourable investment climate by enhancing predictable and stable regulations. In the case of licenses and permits with extended durations, EMnet members and partners emphasised that abrupt changes in regulations and taxation policies can erode investor confidence. Thus, ensuring predictability is paramount to establishing a stable market environment and mitigating risks arising from the disparity between technological advancements and the pace of regulatory development. EMnet members and partners also identified issues related to prolonged waiting periods for permits from governmental bodies and structural deficiencies within regulatory frameworks, especially concerning support for capital-intensive projects. Furthermore, EMnet members and partners underscored how international organisations can play a critical role in defining ethical parameters, pricing standards and regulatory frameworks. EMnet companies indicated how a stable fiscal policy framework could also create the necessary incentives for foreign direct investment (FDI) to flow into emerging markets and accelerate the creation and development of value-added industries.

Enhance risk intelligence, data production and data sharing

Promote data production and accessibility to help lower capital cost and boost investor confidence

EMnet members and partners recognised that emerging and developing countries still encounter difficulties in collecting high-frequency macro-economic and project-level data. These data gaps often increase due diligence expenses and further complicate investment evaluations. In the case of Africa, EMnet companies agreed that rating agencies' representation of African countries could be negatively affected by poor data collection, and the ongoing discussion around establishing an African credit rating agency within the African Union seeks to address this issue (African Union, 2022[3]) (World Economic Forum, 2023[4]). A targeted approach to acquiring further sector-specific data at a granular level is needed in order to better estimate the feasibility of projects and likely return on investment. Despite the ongoing challenges in data collection, EMnet members and partners emphasised a perceptible shift in investors' scrutiny, moving towards evaluating individual countries and projects rather than adopting a generic view of regional contexts. Recognising the role of data production and accessibility in encouraging investment in emerging economies, the OECD and the African Union Commission (AUC) will soon jointly launch a virtual platform dedicated to investment in Africa (see Box 2.1).

Improve data sharing between public and private actors

EMnet members and partners emphasised the importance of data and information sharing between private and public stakeholders in order to inform sound policy measures and foster dialogue with investors. Such measures should be used to target social and environmental challenges and to enhance economic development. In the context of the green transition, EMnet members and partners highlighted that better data availability on emissions could encourage behavioural changes from companies and citizens alike, as well as foster consensus on the main challenges for climate adaptation and mitigation, the reduction of emissions and the protection of biodiversity. International organisations play an important role in facilitating data exchange and providing guidelines to market actors in emerging contexts. For example, the OECD's regional capacity building programme on due diligence for Responsible Business Conduct (RBC) in Latin America informs companies and associations about the tools and techniques required to adopt RBC best practices, including OECD sectoral due diligence instruments and international standards that can be applied in the region (OECD, 2023[5]). In the field of gender equality, EMnet members and partners emphasised that policy action can be better informed by utilising the strengths and resources of both the private and public sectors to produce and analyse more high-quality gender data. International certification and standards, coupled with an effective reporting system for data collection, are important elements in mitigating gender disparities. Sharing gender data among companies and utilising existing cross-country measures through social institutions, such as the OECD Development Centre's Social Institutions and Gender Index (SIGI) (OECD, 2023[6]), can provide valuable insights into the hidden drivers of gender discrimination.

Share success stories to mitigate risk perception

Prevailing risk perception and information gaps can adversely impact investor confidence and heighten the cost of capital. EMnet members and partners agreed that reducing risk perception amid global geopolitical tensions and local uncertainties would substantially help increase investment in emerging markets, where multinational enterprises could underscore heterogeneous experiences. Amplifying success stories can also shift the private sector's perception of the viability of green projects in such contexts, serving as a powerful tool to boost investor confidence, although conducting adequate risk assessments in developing markets remains challenging. Furthermore, EMnet members and partners emphasised that strengthening investment protection instruments can help mitigate the risks associated with investing in financial tools such as ESG-linked instruments, which could help lower investors' risk perception.

Box 2.1. The African Union Commission and the OECD's *African Virtual Investment Platform*

The African Union Commission (AUC) and the OECD are collaboratively working towards establishing the *African Virtual Investment Platform* (AfVIP), a tool designed to catalyse sustainable investment for Africa's productive transformation and job creation. As this development continues, African countries will need to rely less on external development assistance and more on investment, both from within and outside of Africa. Therefore, the Platform aims to support African governments in overcoming key challenges associated with the mobilisation and impact assessment of investments in three ways:

- Enhancing awareness and knowledge of Africa's priority projects, ensuring a comprehensive grasp of the investment landscape.
- Utilising the convening power and technical expertise of the AUC and OECD, the platform aims to foster the co-creation of timely, comprehensive information on investment, thereby facilitating informed decision making.
- Facilitating dialogue for resource mobilisation among African policy makers and their partners, seeking innovative ways to expedite resource mobilisation for impactful investment projects.

By working closely with government representatives and data providers, the platform will generate detailed information and policy-oriented analyses, focusing on improving the quality and impact of investment in Africa. Its key objectives encompass increasing the availability of information on all investment aspects, adapting and co-creating tools with the AUC and OECD, serving as a reference for enhancing investment strategies and providing technical assistance to enhance transparency.

Planned thematic pillars and activities of the platform

The AfVIP roadmap was discussed at the OECD Investment Committee (13 April 2023), at the DEV Governing Board meeting (14 April 2023), at the OECD external committee meeting (May 2023), and at the OECD Council (13 September 2023). It received positive feedback and support from many countries. Under the leadership of the AUC, the roadmap was also discussed and endorsed by the African Union member states at the African Union Ministerial meeting (Specialised Technical Committee) in July 2023 in Nairobi, Kenya. The platform's planned thematic pillars and activities prioritise specific types of investments in its initial years. These include:

- Boosting foreign direct investment (FDI) that strengthens regional value chains and sustainable development by developing indicators and analyses on FDI impact. The platform aims to enable the assessment of decarbonisation, job creation, inclusivity, innovation, and adherence to global standards such as the AfCFTA provisions and OECD frameworks.
- Mobilising domestic and regional financial resources for investment, with a focus on infrastructure. Aiming to improve data on domestic and regional financial resources for investment it will analyse trends, success stories, and investment ecosystems, particularly in productive transformation and regional value-chain development, and infrastructure and energy investments.

Source: (AUC/OECD, n.d.[7]), *African Virtual Investment Platform* (forthcoming).

Box 2.2. Examples of initiatives from the private sector to promote data production and sharing

- **Bayer Crop Science** has partnered with Microsoft to develop cloud-based enterprise solutions that promote innovation and transparency in the agri-food industry. The collaboration aims to enhance data-driven decision making, optimise agricultural processes, and foster sustainable practices to meet the evolving needs of the sector.
- **Mastercard** has developed a Carbon Calculator, that allows users to estimate their carbon footprint based on their purchases. The personalised calculator tracks the carbon footprint monthly across spending categories. It aims at supporting and encouraging positive change by providing tips on how to reduce an individual's carbon footprint through more mindful spending.
- **MUFG Bank** has collaborated with the Monetary Authority of Singapore in developing "Project Greenprint", an integrated digital platform that harnesses technology to simplify how the financial sector and real economy collect, access and act upon environmental, social and governance (ESG) data to support their sustainability initiatives. The collaboration aims to offer an enhanced digital reporting solution for both large businesses and small and medium-sized enterprises (SMEs) to seamlessly report their ESG information.
- **ProFuturo,** a programme developed by Fundación Telefónica and Fundación Bancaria "La Caixa", analyses data to monitor and evaluate the results of its educational programme, a project which has reached 39 countries, benefiting more than 1.2 million children and 334 000 teachers in primary education centres in vulnerable environments across Africa and Latin America, among other regions.

Source: (Bayer, 2023[8]), *Bayer collaborates with Microsoft to unveil new cloud-based enterprise solutions, advancing innovation and transparency in the agri-food industry*, https://www.bayer.com/media/en-us/bayer-collaborates-with-microsoft-to-unveil-new-cloud-based-enterprise-solutions-advancing-innovation-and-transparency-in-the-agri-food-industry/ (accessed on 11 January 2024), (Mastercard, n.d.[9]), *Carbon Calculator: turn purchases into meaningful action*, https://www.mastercard.us/en-us/vision/corp-responsibility/priceless-planet/carbon-calculator.html (accessed on 11 Janaury 2024), (MUFG Bank Ltd, 2023[10]), *MUFG reiterates commitment to unleash further digital transformation in Asia Pacific during Singapore FinTech Festival*, https://www.bk.mufg.jp/global/globalnetwork/asiapacific/anncts/pdf/apacnews-20231117-01-en.pdf (accessed on 31 May 2024), (Profuturo, 2023[11]), *Profuturo Education*, https://profuturo.education/ (accessed on 31 May 2024).

Promote sustainable practices to create long-term value

Align portfolios with socially responsible practices

EMnet members and partners acknowledged that investors are seeking to align their portfolios with socially responsible practices, whether for long-term value creation or the pursuit of a balanced approach between financial and social returns. The ability of these investors to make well-informed decisions depends on the availability of reliable ESG metrics that adhere to recognised international standards. These metrics should encompass a range of factors, including reducing carbon intensity, promoting gender diversity in corporate boards, and ensuring responsible supply chain management. In this regard, EMnet members and partners highlighted three key levers to optimise socially responsible practices: further developing sustainable financial markets, promoting the harmonisation of frameworks and standards for ESG criteria, and developing ESG strategies that incorporate a gender lens and engage top management. The OECD launched a policy paper at the 2022 OECD Forum on Green Finance and Investment, which proposes recommendations to strengthen ESG investment and to accelerate financing of the green transition. This document provides guidance for policy makers and market actors to strengthen ESG investment through the use of quality metrics, rating targets, and frameworks (OECD, 2022[12]). Furthermore, the OECD has developed the Guidelines for Multinational Enterprises on Responsible Business Conduct, providing government recommendations to multinationals on all critical areas of business responsibility, including human rights, labour rights, environmental protection, and anti-bribery and corruption practices. In 2023, the OECD updated these guidelines, expanding the recommendations in key areas like climate change, biodiversity, technology, business integrity, and supply chain due diligence (OECD, 2023[13]).

Adopt a gender lens to investment in emerging markets

Recognising the setbacks caused by the COVID-19 pandemic on development and gender equality, EMnet members and partners considered it both morally imperative and financially beneficial for market actors to adopt a gender lens approach to investment. Gender lens investing, as defined by the OECD, involves incorporating gender analysis into financial decision making, to generate positive outcomes and sustainable development impact for women and girls. FDI can lead to shifts in the relative demand for labour by gender, impacting employment opportunities and wages of women and men differently. Additionally, FDI can influence other aspects of gender equality and women's empowerment in the labour market, such as job security, occupational health, and safety. It can also affect women's access to skills development and career advancement opportunities (OECD, 2022[14]).Gender lens investing typically entails investing in women-owned or women-led enterprises, promoting workplace equity and supporting enterprises that enhance the well-being of women and girls through their products or services (OECD, 2022[15]).

Corporate culture also plays a key role in shaping the gender employment practices of MNEs and is heavily influenced by the values and norms of the MNE's country of origin. Affiliates of MNEs headquartered in more gender-equal countries tend to be more gender-inclusive than domestic firms (OECD, 2022[14]). EMnet members and partners emphasised the significance of public commitment with specific targets that reflect a gender lens across all aspects of business operations. They stressed that gender equality should not be a mere "tick the box" exercise within ESG strategies but rather a fundamental component of a company's strategy for enhancing productivity and fostering innovation.

Encourage circular business models

EMnet members and partners emphasised the importance of incentivising circular business models, adopting innovative financial tools and implementing Key Performance Indicators to monitor sustainability performance across value chains. Encouraging suppliers to align with sustainable development goals and creating markets for sustainable goods and services at all levels of the value chain can play a key role in driving this transition. The potential exists to establish circular business models led by the private sector and adapt agriculture towards a more sustainable future, helping to solve historical economic differences between rural and urban areas (OECD, 2023[16]). EMnet members and partners suggested that using fiscal policies that are sustainable and compatible with green transitions and phasing out environmentally harmful subsidies could provide the necessary support for the private sector to achieve sustainability objectives. In order to provide policy guidance on resource efficiency and accelerate the transition to a circular economy, the OECD has launched the "Resource Efficiency and Circular Economy" (RE-CIRCLE) project. It aims to measure the impact of circular economy policies and to provide qualitative and quantitative analysis to stakeholders in OECD countries and a number of emerging market economies (OECD, n.d.[17]).

Implement sustainable finance mechanisms

Sustainable finance experienced setbacks in 2022 due to significant monetary tightening; however, a rebound is now expected. The analysis points towards an increase in financial instruments, such as GSSS bonds, which were projected to reach a value between USD 900 billion and USD 1 trillion in 2023 (S&P, 2023[18]). In this context, EMnet members and partners emphasised the importance of implementing sustainable finance mechanisms for the green transition in emerging markets. Blended finance instruments, as well as GSSS bonds, could enhance access to liquidity and promote more investments in green infrastructure projects. However, understanding and evaluating the economic value of these financial instruments remains challenging. EMnet members and partners stressed the importance of developing sound, sustainable financial mechanisms and providing clear guidelines and incentives for accessing these. Furthermore, governments and policy makers are increasingly acknowledging the significance of implementing effective ESG standards, as well as enhancing transparency around sustainable investment products. The European Union, for instance, is multiplying the number of regulations related to sustainability in business operations, such as the Sustainable Finance Disclosure Regulation, among many others (Eurosif, n.d.[19]). EMnet members and partners stressed that to encourage more investment in ESG-linked instruments in emerging economies, market infrastructure needs to be improved by diversifying the investor base, reinforcing investment protection instruments, and advocating for common taxonomies across regions. For example, strengthening investment protection instruments can help mitigate the risks associated with investing in ESG-linked instruments, which could improve investors' perception of risk. Discussions showed how progress is already being made to ensure that sustainable finance mechanisms and instruments incorporate concerns from shareholders, investors, and consumers, such as safeguards included in ESG loans, climate bonds and blended finance. Emerging economies are progressing at a fast pace in the field of sustainable finance. In the LAC region, between 2012 and 2021, corporate green finance reached over USD 40 billion in Argentina, Brazil, Colombia, Ecuador and Mexico – making them five of the world's top 20 destination countries for green transition financing. The region received 17% of global private green finance, equivalent to USD 8.5 billion, between 2018 and 2020 (OECD et al., 2022[20]).

Box 2.3. Examples of initiatives from the private sector to promote sustainable practices in emerging and developing economies

- **BBVA** issued, in September 2023, the first sustainable corporate bond to Hochschild Mining Corporation in Peru. The aim is to foster a responsible corporate culture that contributes to environmental, social and governance (ESG) issues and encourages behavioural change within the private sector.
- **MUFG Bank** concluded, in March 2023, the second-largest global social loan for the State Bank of India, equivalent to USD 1 billion, to finance social projects, such as affordable housing and lending for small and medium-sized businesses. This includes support for women entrepreneurs, micro-entrepreneurs, self-help and joint liability groups, and smallholder farms.

Source: (BBVA, 2023[21]), *BBVA grants the first sustainable corporate loan to a mining company in Peru*, www.bbva.com/en/sustainability/bbva-grants-the-first-sustainable-corporate-loan-to-a-mining-company-in-peru/ (accessed on 11 January 2024), (DHL, n.d.[22]), *Breaking down barriers to global trade*, www.dhl.com/global-en/delivered/sustainability/gotrade-program.html (accessed on 11 January 2024), (MUFG Bank Ltd, 2023[23]), *MUFG concludes landmark USD 1 billion social loan for State Bank of India*, https://www.bk.mufg.jp/global/globalnetwork/asiapacific/anncts/pdf/apacnews-20230301-01-en.pdf (accessed on 11 January 2024).

Enable collaboration between multinational enterprises and local SMEs

Design sustainability requirements in line with SME capacities

To foster workable sustainable practices in supply chains, it is essential to adjust sustainability targets, regulations and frameworks to fit the capacity of SMEs. EMnet members and partners recognised the unique challenges faced by SMEs, such as limited resources and capabilities, and stressed the importance of designing sustainability measures that are feasible and proportionate for them. This requires tailoring sustainability targets to the size and capabilities of SMEs and ensuring that they can realistically meet and integrate them into their operations. Additionally, streamlining regulatory requirements, simplifying compliance procedures, and providing clear guidance can support SMEs in understanding and complying with international sustainability standards. At COP26, the OECD launched its Platform on Financing SMEs for Sustainability in order to advance knowledge sharing, data and analytical work, and policy dialogue on sustainable finance for SMEs. This platform brings together governments, financial institutions, regulators, and SME representatives to develop solutions and good practices (OECD, n.d.[24]).

Support SMEs to progress in digital and green transitions

To ensure a fair and inclusive green transition, EMnet members and partners recommended supporting SMEs in agribusiness and other emerging industries. SMEs are crucial economic players as they employ most of the working population in developing countries. Consequently, the population in emerging countries are often highly vulnerable to the effects of climate change due to their high dependence on SMEs in agribusiness and natural resource exploitation. Therefore, governments need to implement adequate policies to address the financial and technical needs of SMEs and to introduce more digital and greener technologies, which can have a positive impact at the local level within these countries. In many emerging and developing economies, SMEs are lagging behind the digital transition, missing the potential benefits in productivity brought by an effective use of digital technologies. Digitalisation can also help with the long-term goals of creating more formal jobs and increasing fiscal revenues. EMnet members and partners stressed the importance of public-private collaboration to increase access to digital technologies for SMEs and rural businesses. Public-private collaboration should also address the issue of access to finance for SMEs, particularly female entrepreneurs and women-led businesses.

Promote market linkages and increase financial support for SMEs

Quality FDI can benefit emerging economies through knowledge and technology spillovers that increase the productivity of domestic SMEs (OECD, 2023[25]). EMnet members and partners highlighted a significant shift in focus, post the COVID-19 pandemic, towards prioritising investment retention, aftercare services, and investment facilitation in emerging and developing economies. EMnet members and partners also emphasised the necessity of aligning policies aimed at attracting FDI with the interests of local actors, especially SMEs, by introducing incentives and policies tailored to support local businesses. An open, transparent, and non-discriminatory regulatory environment is crucial for attracting FDI that fosters linkages with the host economy. To maximise the benefits of FDI, governments should enhance the diffusion channels of FDI-SME spillovers by encouraging value chain linkages and strategic partnerships between FDI and domestic SMEs. This can be achieved through initiatives such as supplier development programmes or incentive schemes targeting foreign investors (OECD, 2023[25]). Furthermore, private equity funds can play a pivotal role in deciding to invest in SMEs, enabling local companies to scale up their business, such as through new hires and plant expansions. However, some emerging economies, especially in Africa, still face challenges in attracting FDI, primarily due to their struggle to compete on a global playing field, often characterised by lower liquidity and are overall less attractive to investors compared to other regions (AUC/OECD, 2023[26]).

Box 2.4. Examples of initiatives from the private sector to support small and medium-sized enterprises (SMEs)

- **AeTrade Group**'s Strategic Investment Alliance was created as an inclusive platform for investors with a common vision to channel finance towards micro, small and medium-sized enterprises (MSMEs) in line with the principles endorsed by the African Union. The Alliance is a "pooled fund" that seeks to attract both impact and sustainable investments to stimulate job creation and inclusive growth for MSMEs in economic sectors, including business products and services (business-to-business [B2B]), utilities, infrastructure, industrial, digitalisation and manufacturing.
- **DHL**'s GoTrade sustainability programme builds on the United Nations' Sustainable Development Goals to increase the number and volume of SMEs in developing countries trading across borders thanks to capacity building and partnerships with international organisations. This is particularly important when it comes to emerging markets, where SMEs are responsible for the generation of seven out of ten formal jobs.
- **MUFG Bank, the Asian Institute of Digital Finance (AIDF), CriAT and iAPPS-FundON** have jointly developed GreenON – the first ever digital service which uses data to analyse the initiatives of food companies and agri-producers against their sustainability objectives. The platform provides timely and verifiable sector-specific green data for environmental impact assessment. This will also help mobilise green capital for desired projects with improved information transparency.

Source: (AeTrade Group, 2023[27]), *Africa Strategic Alliance*, www.aetradegroup.com/post/africa-strategic-investment-alliance (accessed on 11 January 2024), (DHL, n.d.[22]), *Breaking down barriers to global trade*, www.dhl.com/global-en/delivered/sustainability/gotrade-program.html (accessed on 11 January 2024), (MUFG Bank Ltd, 2021[28]), *"GreenON" is Asia's first digital service that lists green credentials of agri-producers under development*, https://www.bk.mufg.jp/global/globalnetwork/asiapacific/anncts/pdf/apacnews-20211109-01_en.pdf (accessed on 31 May 2024).

Foster development by building public-private partnerships

Improve infrastructure by leveraging on public-private partnerships

Public-private dialogue should result in stable investment policy frameworks, more long-term infrastructure investment and sound fiscal policies. EMnet members and partners highlighted the transformative potential of public-private partnerships in conceiving and executing large-scale green infrastructure projects and aligning efforts to combat climate change. Drawing inspiration from successful models, such as the EU Global Gateway, collaborative investment with the private sector in innovation, infrastructure, and clean technologies becomes a pivotal element in steering sustainable growth within emerging and developing economies. Conceived as the Pan-European strategy to boost infrastructure and strengthen health, education and research systems in LAC, the Middle East, Asia and the Pacific, and Sub-Saharan Africa, the Global Gateway aims at mobilising up to EUR 300 billion in mixed investments in the coming years (European Commission, n.d.[29]). In addition, by promoting special economic zones (SEZs), local governments in developing countries can hope to attract foreign investment more effectively and thus overcome structural infrastructure gaps. By developing SEZs, policy makers aim to strengthen the economic development of their countries, especially in lagging regions. Goals include more foreign investment, higher exports and job creation. Importantly, SEZ policies show an increasing focus on indirectly fostering the growth of local industries for greater productivity (UNCTAD, 2021[30]).

Recognise the private sector's support of local communities

Three main stakeholder groups – companies, governments and communities – must co-ordinate their efforts to further advance sustainable development. Collaboration between governments and local communities and the adoption of mechanisms such as concessions and royalties offer multiple pathways for public-private partnerships and risk mitigation. Multinational companies play a crucial role by tailoring sustainable business models to local contexts, aligning strategies with community needs, capitalising on regional comparative advantages, and forming partnerships with local suppliers and stakeholders. This approach ensures inclusive value chains and creates a conducive environment for knowledge and technology sharing. EMnet members and partners stressed the importance of taking into account the social repercussions of the triple (green, social and digital) transition. This involves addressing the needs of vulnerable groups, paying attention to territories and communities, and prioritising the creation of quality, formal jobs. The effects on the labour market stemming from the green and digital transitions will demand policies that facilitate the reskilling of workers, generate new job opportunities, particularly in rural areas, and provide support to displaced workers and their communities, among other measures. As much as 10.5% net jobs could be created in LAC by 2030 with the green and just transition (OECD et al., 2023[31]). By systematically promoting diversity, inclusion and capacity building through education and training, EMnet members and partners recognised the important challenges and investment associated with workforce training programmes for reskilling and upskilling but also recognised the potential of equipping employees with the necessary knowledge of sustainability and circular business models. EMnet members and partners considered strengthening digital capacity-building efforts an important opportunity, not only to improve digital skills but also to enhance the economic situation of underserved populations. Public and private stakeholders should, therefore, focus on providing relevant and accessible education on digital transformation, financial inclusion and the use of digital tools to all individuals. Capacity-building activities can take the form of training programmes, workshops, and educational campaigns, and all members and partners emphasised the prioritisation of underserved groups such as women, youth and small businesses in these training initiatives.

Align investment with public policy objectives

EMnet members and partners stressed that public-private dialogue is an integral part of the green, social and digital transition, as it is essential to break silos, promote a whole-of-government co-ordination of policy initiatives and involve key external stakeholders. Additionally, governments should promote a constant and flexible dialogue with the private sector, aiming to develop realistic policies that are aligned with the companies' business capacities and market goals. Without this approach, EMnet members and partners acknowledged that governments may fail to align with the realities of companies and other market actors, thus discouraging further investment and hindering the achievement of climate goals. EMnet members and partners highlighted the need for an alignment between public and private sectors, particularly in areas such as skills development, investment in information and communication technologies and investment regulations. EMnet members and partners encouraged policy makers to actively seek private sector input through consultations, to draw from their experience and leverage their competencies. International organisations can also play a key role in setting common standards to align investment with public policy objectives. The OECD introduced in 2022 a recommendation of the Council on FDI Qualities for Sustainable Development, aiming to support governments in maximising FDI contribution to sustainable development in the areas of productivity and innovation, job quality and skills, gender equality, and decarbonisation. Additionally, it recommends that governments strengthen FDI's positive impact in developing countries, also by increasing engagement with the private sector and promote multi-stakeholder partnerships (OECD, 2022[32]).

Box 2.5. Examples of initiatives from the private sector to enhance public-private partnerships

- **American Tower Corporation** (ATC) has launched more than 300 digital communities since 2012 in 8 countries and has committed to building a further 2 000 communities over the next 5 years. These sites, with broadband connectivity and uninterrupted power, aim to increase digital inclusion and access to digital services, providing skills training for jobs, as well as health and financial services to underserved communities, in particular women who do not have access to Information and Communication Technology (ICT) training.
- **Enel** launched a "Hoja de Ruta" programme as part of the study's roadmap for the energy transition in Latin America from 2030 to 2050. Over 8 countries and 11 000 stakeholders were included in the study, and they contributed through 24 workshops and more than 50 sessions.
- **Bayer Crop Science**'s *Better Life Farming (BLF) Alliance* helps smallholder farmers and their communities by providing green solutions, information on good agricultural practices, on-farm training and market access, to help them unlock their full potential and promote the development of sustainable farming businesses.
- **Telefónica**'s alliance with *Comunidad Andina de Naciones* (CAN) recently launched the *Conecta Empleo* project specifically for CAN citizens in search of employment. People who wish to improve their employability and/or digital skills can access this platform and find free online courses to develop the digital skills currently in demand by employers. To date, the *Conecta Empleo* platform, as a whole, has benefited over 277 000 people through its virtual referrer.
- **DHL** signed a Memorandum of Understanding with UNIDO in the framework of the 28th UN Climate Change Conference, committing to minimise food waste and shift the paradigms around agriculture, and launched the "Innovation for Food Systems Transformation" global innovation challenge. This partnership aims to enhance food preservation, reduce food waste in African markets, and improve global market accessibility for producers. DHL Group has also teamed up with the International Trade Center's "SheTrades" initiative to support and train women-led businesses. The initiative has reached over 1 300 attendees from SMEs in African countries, of which 92% were women.

Source: (American Tower Corporation, 2024[33]), *Digital Communities*, www.americantower.com/digital-communities (accessed on 12 January 2024), (ENEL, 2022[34]), *Se presentaron los resultados del estudio "Hoja de ruta para la transición energética en Colombia 2050"*, http://enel.com.co/content/dam/enel-co/espa%C3%B1ol/7-prensa/2022/noviembre/resultados-hoja-de-ruta/se-presentaron-los-resultados-del-estudio-hoja-de-ruta-para-la-transicion-energetica-en-colombia-2050.pdf (accessed on 12 January 2024), (Better Life Farming, n.d.[35]), *Empowering smallholder farmers with resources for a brighter future*, https://www.betterlifefarming.com/who-we-are/ (accessed on 26 March 2024), (Fundación Telefónica, 2024[36]), *General Secretariat of the Andean Community and Fundación Telefónica launch 19 free courses for the development of digital skills and competencies*, https://www.comunidadandina.org/tag/conecta-empleo/ (accessed on 31 May 2024), (Fundación Telefónica, 2023[37]), *Conecta Empleo has more than 17,500 people trained in digital skills in Spain and 277,000 globally*, https://www.fundaciontelefonica.com/noticias/cifras-conecta-empleo-2023/ (accessed on 31 May 2023), (DHL Group, 2023[38]), *UNIDO and DHL Group join forces to tackle food waste and climate impact*, https://group.dhl.com/en/media-relations/press-releases/2023/unido-and-dhl-group-join-forces-to-tackle-food-waste-and-climate-impact.html (accessed on 31 May 2024), (ITC, n.d.[39]), *SheTrades Partner*, https://www.shetrades.com/partners/ (accessed on 25 March 2024).

References

AeTrade Group (2023), *Africa Strategic Investment Alliance*, http://aetradegroup.com/post/africa-strategic-investment-alliance (accessed on 11 January 2024). [27]

African Union (2022), *Ghana Supports the Establishment of the African Credit Rating Agency*, https://au.int/en/pressreleases/20220720/ghana-supports-establishment-african-credit-rating-agency (accessed on 10 January 2024). [3]

American Tower Corporation (2024), *Digital Communities*, http://americantower.com/digital-communities (accessed on 12 January 2024). [33]

AUC/OECD (2023), *Africa's Development Dynamics 2023: Investing in Sustainable Development*, African Union Commission, Addis Ababa/OECD Publishing, Paris, https://doi.org/10.1787/3269532b-en. [26]

AUC/OECD (n.d.), *African Virtual Investment Platform (forthcoming)*. [7]

Bayer (2023), *Bayer collaborates with Microsoft to unveil new cloud-based enterprise solutions, advancing innovation and transparency in the agri-food industry*, https://www.bayer.com/media/en-us/bayer-collaborates-with-microsoft-to-unveil-new-cloud-based-enterprise-solutions-advancing-innovation-and-transparency-in-the-agri-food-industry/ (accessed on 11 January 2024). [8]

BBVA (2023), *BBVA grants the first sustainable corporate loan to a mining company in Peru*, http://bbva.com/en/sustainability/bbva-grants-the-first-sustainable-corporate-loan-to-a-mining-company-in-peru/ (accessed on 11 January 2024). [21]

Better Life Farming (n.d.), *Empowering smallholder farmers with resources for a brighter future*, https://www.betterlifefarming.com/who-we-are/ (accessed on 26 March 2024). [35]

DHL (n.d.), *Breaking down barriers to global trade*, http://dhl.com/global-en/delivered/sustainability/gotrade-program.html (accessed on 11 January 2024). [22]

DHL Group (2023), *UNIDO and DHL Group join forces to tackle food waste and climate impact*, https://group.dhl.com/en/media-relations/press-releases/2023/unido-and-dhl-group-join-forces-to-tackle-food-waste-and-climate-impact.html (accessed on 31 May 2024). [38]

ENEL (2022), *Se presentaron los resultados del estudio "Hoja de ruta para la transición energética en Colombia 2050"*, http://enel.com.co/content/dam/enel-co/espa%C3%B1ol/7-prensa/2022/noviembre/resultados-hoja-de-ruta/se-presentaron-los-resultados-del-estudio-hoja-de-ruta-para-la-transicion-energetica-en-colombia-2050.pdf (accessed on 12 January 2024). [34]

European Commission (n.d.), *Global Gateway*, http://international-partnerships.ec.europa.eu/policies/global-gateway_en (accessed on 11 January 2024). [29]

Eurosif (n.d.), *SFDR*, https://www.eurosif.org/policies/sfdr/ (accessed on 11 January 2024). [19]

Fundación Telefónica (2024), *General Secretariat of the Andean Community and Fundación Telefónica launch 19 free courses for the development of digital skills and competencies*, https://www.comunidadandina.org/tag/conecta-empleo/ (accessed on 31 May 2024). [36]

Fundación Telefónica (2023), *Conecta Empleo has more than 17,500 people trained in digital skills in Spain and 277,000 globally*, https://www.fundaciontelefonica.com/noticias/cifras-conecta-empleo-2023/ (accessed on 31 May 2023). [37]

ITC (n.d.), *SheTrades Partner*, https://www.shetrades.com/partners/ (accessed on 25 March 2024). [39]

Mastercard (n.d.), *Carbon Calculator: turn purchases into meaningful action*, https://www.mastercard.us/en-us/vision/corp-responsibility/priceless-planet/carbon-calculator.html (accessed on 11 Janaury 2024). [9]

Ministry of Energy (2022), *Kenya Energy Sector Roadmap 2040*, Ministry of Energy, Nairobi, https://naturaljustice.org/wp-content/uploads/2022/11/Submissions-on-Draft-Kenya-Energy-White-Paper.pdf. [2]

MUFG Bank Ltd (2023), *MUFG concludes landmark USD 1 billion social loan for State Bank of India*, https://www.bk.mufg.jp/global/globalnetwork/asiapacific/anncts/pdf/apacnews-20230301-01-en.pdf (accessed on 11 January 2024). [23]

MUFG Bank Ltd (2023), *MUFG reiterates commitment to unleash further digital transformation in Asia Pacific during Singapore FinTech Festival*, https://www.bk.mufg.jp/global/globalnetwork/asiapacific/anncts/pdf/apacnews-20231117-01-en.pdf (accessed on 31 May 2024). [10]

MUFG Bank Ltd (2021), *"GreenON" is Asia's first digital service that lists green credentials of agri-producers under development*, https://www.bk.mufg.jp/global/globalnetwork/asiapacific/anncts/pdf/apacnews-20211109-01_en.pdf (accessed on 31 May 2024). [28]

OECD (2023), *Business Insights on Emerging Markets 2023*, OECD Publishing, Paris, https://www.oecd.org/dev/EMnet-Business-Insights-2023.pdf. [16]

OECD (2023), *OECD Guidelines for Multinational Enterprises on Responsible Business Conduct*, OECD Publishing, Paris, https://doi.org/10.1787/81f92357-en. [5]

OECD (2023), *OECD Guidelines for Multinational Enterprises on Responsible Business Conduct*, OECD Publishing, Paris, https://doi.org/10.1787/81f92357-en. [13]

OECD (2023), *Policy Toolkit for Strengthening FDI and SME Linkages*, OECD Publishing, Paris, https://doi.org/10.1787/688bde9a-en. [25]

OECD (2023), *SIGI 2023 Global Report: Gender Equality in Times of Crisis*, Social Institutions and Gender Index, OECD Publishing, Paris, https://doi.org/10.1787/4607b7c7-en. [6]

OECD (2022), *Development finance for gender equality and women's empowerment: A snapshot*, OECD Publishing, Paris, https://web-archive.oecd.org/2022-05-05/630214-Gender_ODA_2022.pdf. [15]

OECD (2022), *FDI Qualities Policy Toolkit*, OECD Publishing, Paris, https://doi.org/10.1787/7ba74100-en. [14]

OECD (2022), "Policy guidance on market practices to strengthen ESG investing and finance a climate transition", *OECD Business and Finance Policy Papers*, No. 13, OECD Publishing, Paris, https://doi.org/10.1787/2c5b535c-en. [12]

OECD (2022), *Recommendation of the Council on Foreign Direct Investment Qualities for Sustainable Development*, OECD/LEGAL/0476. [32]

OECD (n.d.), *OECD Platform on Financing SMEs for Sustainability*, http://oecd.org/cfe/smes/financing-smes-sustainability.htm (accessed on 11 January 2024). [24]

OECD (n.d.), *RE-CIRCLE: resource efficiency and circular economy*, http://oecd.org/environment/waste/recircle.htm (accessed on 11 January 2024). [17]

OECD et al. (2023), *Latin American Economic Outlook 2023: Investing in Sustainable Development*, OECD Publishing, Paris, https://doi.org/10.1787/8c93ff6e-en. [31]

OECD et al. (2021), *Latin American Economic Outlook 2021: Working Together for a Better Recovery*, OECD Publishing, Paris, https://doi.org/10.1787/5fedabe5-en. [1]

OECD et al. (2022), *Latin American Economic Outlook 2022: Towards a Green and Just Transition*, OECD Publishing, Paris, https://doi.org/10.1787/3d5554fc-en. [20]

Profuturo (2023), *Profuturo Education*, https://profuturo.education/ (accessed on 31 May 2024). [11]

S&P (2023), *Sustainable Bond Issuance Will Return To Growth in 2023*, Standard & Poor's Financial Services, New York, http://spglobal.com/_assets/documents/ratings/research/101572346.pdf. [18]

UNCTAD (2021), *Handbook on Special Economic Zones in Africa: Towards Economic Diversification across the Continent*, United Nations Conference on Trade and Development, Geneva, http://unctad.org/system/files/official-document/diaeia2021d3_en.pdf. [30]

World Economic Forum (2023), *The African Union wants to create its own credit rating agency. Here's why*, http://weforum.org/agenda/2023/10/african-union-au-create-credit-rating-agency-finance-capital/ (accessed on 10 January 2024). [4]

3 Central Bank Digital Currencies: What is in it for emerging markets?

This chapter explores how central banks in emerging markets have been considering or initiating Central Bank Digital Currencies (CBDCs) as a potentially disruptive tool for financial inclusion. The chapter presents case studies for the Bahamas, Brazil, the People's Republic of China, India and Nigeria.

Key messages

- After the 2008-09 global financial crisis, the foundations of modern banking have been challenged. Coupled with rapid advances in financial technology, economies around the world have seen a proliferation of new financial products and processes.
- Most significant global trends include end-to-end digital transformation of financial services in different parts of the world, rapid adoption of digital payments products and more recently, cryptocurrencies and blockchain-enabled products.
- Since 2019, central banks across the world, mainly from emerging markets, have considered or initiated the process of digitising their currencies by introducing some form of Central Bank Digital Currencies (CBDCs).
- CBDCs, if implemented successfully, have the potential to be a disruptive change to the global financial system and a tool for financial inclusion in emerging markets. As countries with volatile currencies are looking for a solution, it is not a surprise that CBDCs have been launched in those contexts.
- Many central banks have produced concept notes and launched pilots across emerging markets. Potential benefits and risks associated with the introduction of CDBCs in these contexts have arisen.
- By exploring some country cases – the Bahamas, Brazil, the People's Republic of China (hereafter "China"), India, and Nigeria – the analysis can shed light on this new phenomenon in the banking system.

Understanding CBDCs

Central Bank Digital Currency (CBDC) refers to a digital form of a country's official currency that is issued and regulated by the country's central bank. It is essentially a digital representation of a nation's fiat currency, such as the US dollar or the Chinese Yuan, that is backed by the central bank and operates within a centralised system (Prasad, 2021[1]). CBDCs are designed to leverage the advantages of digital technology while maintaining the stability and control associated with traditional fiat currencies. They aim to provide a secure and efficient means of conducting digital transactions, both domestically and internationally.

CBDCs are recognised as a form of legal tender, just like physical banknotes and coins. They are created and issued by the central bank, making them a direct liability of the central bank. Consequently, the central bank retains full control over the issuance, supply, and distribution of CBDCs (Prasad, 2021[1]). Such currency exists in electronic form, typically stored in digital wallets or accounts. However, different central banks may design different systems for the storage and transfer of their CBDC.

While multiple countries have proposed their own system of CBDCs, two types of CBDCs are commonly defined – retail and wholesale CBDCs. Retail CBDCs are closest to current cash. Retail CBDCs will be a widely accessible form of digital currency issued by a central bank to the public through tools like e-wallets. China currently has the most advanced pilots for retail CBDCs, with other countries like Sweden and Argentina also having experimented with pilots. Wholesale CBDCs, on the other hand, will be issued by the central bank to facilitate inter-banking transactions for financial institutions. It is estimated that the wholesale CBDCs would be a safer and more efficient form of domestic and cross-border transactions (Prasad, 2021[1]). Singapore, Canada, and France have reached advanced pilot stage for wholesale CBDCs.

We can distinguish three models of governance (or types of architecture). The direct model where the central bank interacts directly with the end users, whether individuals, business or financial institutions, and maintains record of all transactions in a centralised ledger; the intermediated model (or token based model) where the central bank distributes the CBDCs to intermediaries such as banks and other financial institutions that in turn distribute them to the general public; the users hold and transact with the CBDC (the token) directly, without the need for intermediaries to get involved; in this model the central bank has no direct link with the public. The third is the hybrid model. This is a two-tiered model wherein the central bank releases digital currency to retail users and intermediaries with different countries have specific models/versions proposed. Consumers can use the CBDC to carry out retail transactions through intermediaries. Such models provide considerable space for the intermediaries to act as payment co-ordinators and innovate further. India, China and Hong Kong (China) are all trying to pilot and launch such models.

One way in which CBDCs differs from physical cash is through attributes related to their digital nature. For example, CBDCs enables instant transactions for retail and inter-bank transfers, improving efficiency and reducing settlement times. Some CBDC designs include programmable features, allowing for conditional transactions and smart contract functionality.

Ideally, CBDCs should contain strong security measures to prevent counterfeiting and ensure transaction privacy. In particular, privacy and anonymity of a CBDC is something different central banks are struggling to incorporate in their new framework. CBDCs can coexist with physical cash or potentially replace it in the future, depending on the specific implementation and policy objectives of each country.

In emerging markets, CBDCs are often the result of the fast development of mobile payments whose remarkable expansion in these markets is largely due to their low level of bancarisation and to technological development and smartphone penetration, which facilitated the access of the population to a wide range of financial services. It is not a coincidence that besides Alipay and Wechat Pay launched in China in 2004 and 2013 respectively, another early success story is M-Pesa launched in 2007 by Kenya Mobile in a Joint Venture with Vodacom, a South African mobile telecom company, a subsidiary of the British Vodafone and the Central Bank of Kenya.

Global adoption of CBDCs

The concept of a CBDC, though novel, has caught the imagination of central banks and governments across the world in the past decade. For most emerging economies, the potential of CBDCs to improve financial inclusion, cross-border international payments and promote digitisation in their domestic financial sectors has been a key driver of their interest in CBDCs. A broader stimulant has been the rapid mushrooming of private virtual currencies, and the massive influx of investment in such currencies and tokens such as Bitcoin. The drastic fluctuations in the value of crypto assets and transaction volumes have spurred governments to explore novel means of regulation and protection of investors. In addition, through crypto, governments have been confronted with the risk of losing control of their currency, which has always been their prerogative (Mohácsi, 2023[2]). Against this background, an increasing number of central banks and governments across the world have been releasing concept notes and pilots for different models of CBDCs. As of September 2023, 130 countries were considering the launch of a CBDC, almost quadrupling the number of countries in May 2020.

However, as of January 2024, only three countries had a CBDC formally implemented: the Bahamas, Jamaica and Nigeria (see Table 3.1) while others are at the testing phase. China, for instance, having begun research on CBDCs in 2014, has crossed a second pilot stage for the introduction of the Chinese CBDC, the e-Yuan (Jahan, 2022[3])in some cities and during events like the Winter Olympics in February 2022.

Other countries are proceeding more cautiously, weighing the potential benefits against risks such as financial stability, privacy and cybersecurity. The European Central Bank (ECB), for instance, has been actively researching CBDCs but has not yet made a firm decision on their implementation. The US is ambivalent about the usefulness of a digital dollar (Carapella, 2024[4]). The US Federal Reserve has been conducting research on a US CBDC (Flemming, 2024[5]). It has organised public discussion with stakeholders, publishing in January 2022 a paper inviting public comments on the matter (US Federal Reserve, 2022[6]).

Table 3.1. Countries with CBDCs: Selected emerging economies

Country	Nigeria	Brazil	China	India	Russia	Indonesia	Thailand	Bahamas	Jamaica
Country group	E20+1	E20+1	E20+1	E20+1	E20+1	E20+1	E20+1	Other	Other
Status	Launched	Pilot	Pilot	Pilot	Pilot	Development	Pilot	Launched	Launched
Architecture	Intermediated	Intermediated	Intermediated	Intermediated	Intermediated	Undecided	Intermediated	Intermediated	Intermediated
Use case	Retail	Retail/ Wholesale	Retail/ Wholesale	Retail/ Wholesale	Retail/ Wholesale	Retail/ Wholesale	Retail/ Wholesale	Retail	Retail

Note: *E20+1 is a group of 20 top emerging economies plus China established by EMI (Casanova and Miroux, 2023[7]) .
Source: Authors and Kaleb Kavuma, based on data from Atlantic Council, Central Bank Currency Digital Currency Tracker, https://www.atlanticcouncil.org/cbdctracker/, accessed in March 2024.

While progress has been made, the journey towards a widespread adoption of CBDCs is complex, involving a variety of technical, regulatory and even societal issues. The challenges faced are illustrated by the Caribbean Union that launched its own CBDC in 2021 and had to interrupt it for technical reasons in 2022. Since then, the Union has been working on a 2.0 version of its CBDC that may be launched in 2024.

CBDCs in emerging markets: Some case studies

To date, the trend is led by emerging markets. The following explores a few country case studies: China and India in Asia, Brazil and Bahamas in Latin America and Nigeria in Africa, highlighting the issues involved in implementing a CBDC.

China: "e-Yuan" in the spotlight

Given its size and role in the global economy, China has been at the forefront of the CBDC experiment, launching its pilot phase in 2019. China's CBDC is known as the Digital Currency Electronic Payment (DCEP), also referred to as the Digital Yuan or e-CNY. Its implementation has been driven by the government's aim to modernise the country's payment system, enhance financial inclusion, and reinforce its control over the monetary system. The Digital Yuan is issued and controlled by the People's Bank of China. It is stored in digital wallets, which can be held by individuals, businesses, or financial institutions. Users can access their digital yuans and use them in transactions through designated mobile apps or other supported platforms, including the two main Chinese payment platforms Alipay and WeChat Pay that have now integrated the digital yuan app (Nambiampurath, 2023[8]).

The digital yuan operates on a two-tier system where the central bank issues the digital currency to commercial banks and other authorised institutions, which then distribute it to the public. This approach ensures wider acceptance and compatibility with existing financial infrastructure. One notable feature of the e-CNY is the ability to conduct transactions even offline, using near-field communication (NFC) technology. This feature facilitates peer-to-peer transfers without relying on internet connectivity.

China has conducted extensive pilot programmes for the e-CNY in various cities and regions to test its functionality, user experience, and potential use cases. These pilot programmes have involved collaborations with commercial banks, e-commerce platforms, and other entities. While official numbers are unavailable, the total number of e-CNY wallets reportedly reached 261 million in 2021, with total transactions of RMB 88 billion or about USD 13.8 billion, still a negligible fraction of the total money supply in China despite the reportedly large number of wallets (Jahan, 2022[3]). As of 2024, the pilot wants to optimise overseas tourist use and expand cross-border applications of e-CNY (Atlantic Council, n.d.[9]).

"E-Rupee" – India's CBDC: Building on UPI's success launched in 2016

India has been pushing for a major transformation of its payment ecosystem with the launch of its digital payment platform (the Unified Payment Interface or UPI) in 2016. Its rapid adoption has been instrumental in boosting digital payments. Launching a CBDC, the e-Rupee, would be another key step towards a digital economy.

The Reserve Bank of India (RBI) has two primary objectives driving the design of the e-Rupee – to create a digital currency that mirrors paper currency, and to manage the introduction and adoption of the digital currency in a seamless manner (Reserve Bank of India, 2022[10]). As in other countries, key concerns revolve around financial stability, security, and consumer protection. Particular attention is also being paid to privacy. While legislative means are being considered for this purpose, the Indian central bank is also reportedly exploring technology to address privacy risks (Singh, 2024[11]).

In December 2022, the RBI launched the pilot for retail e-Rupee. As of February 2023, this pilot project was deployed in five cities within closed user groups on an invitation-basis only (Gandhi, 2023[12]). As of early 2024, there was no official deadline for the formal implementation of the e-Rupee in India. Interoperability, a key objective of the RBI, including through integration with payments platform, is essential in the widespread adoption of CBDCs. In that respect, India can build upon the success of UPI that in 2022 registered over 74 billion transactions and 126 Indian rupee trillions (about USD 510 billion).

"E-Naira" – Nigeria's CBDC: At a crossroads

E-Naira, Nigeria's CBDC initiative, was released in October 2021 to widespread interest. As in other cases, the aim of the e-Naira was to drive financial inclusion, enhance the current payment systems, and mitigate against the dollarisation of the economy. Facilitating cross border transaction was important, given the importance of diaspora remittances for the economy. However, as of October 2022, the level of adoption within the country full of crypto-curious investors remained very low, even as paper Naira notes are in short supply in the country. One year after the launch of the e-naira, less than 0.5% of the population had used it. The number of wallets downloaded was 860 000 but an estimated 98% were deemed inactive (Jahan, 2022[3]), and the volume of transactions had reached USD 9.3 million, compared to USD 26 billion for ATM cash withdrawals in 2020. Following the severe cash shortage encouraged by Nigeria government in 2022, with limitations on cash withdrawals, the volume of retail transactions reportedly rose to an estimated USD 48 billion by July 2023 (EOS Intelligence, 2024[13]).

There are several reasons for the relatively low adoption of the e-naira including the devaluation of the naira and lack of trust in the technology. They also include infrastructure challenges (internet access and electricity supply for instance), and the need to enhance consumers' education, as well as staff training to facilitate users' onboarding. Interoperability with existing payment platforms has also faced challenges, constituting an additional barrier to adoption.

Bahamas, a pioneer experiment

The Bahamian Sand Dollar is the official Central Bank Digital Currency (CBDC) of The Bahamas. It was launched by the Central Bank in October 2020, making The Bahamas the first country in the world to introduce a fully operational CBDC.

Operating as a digital version of the existing fiat currency, and accessed through a mobile wallet application, the Bahamas Sand Dollar functions alongside physical banknotes and coins. Similar motivations as those applying in other emerging economies that launched or are testing CBDCs apply.

The Bahamian Sand Dollar is pegged to the US dollar; it cannot be used for cross-border transactions. Three years after it was launched, the sand dollar had reached USD 2.1 million in circulation, i.e. less than 0.5% of cash in circulation in the country. The need to educate consumers on the use of the Sand dollar is a barrier to adoption, as in other countries. The importance of the informal sector in the economy also plays a role as well as the deficiencies of internet infrastructure in several islands. To address this challenge, the central bank has been working on CBDC that could also be used offline. On privacy, as per the Central Bank, only banks and Payment service providers have access to the users' identity; the latter will be known to the central bank only if there is an investigation for criminal activity (Ledger Insights, n.d.[14]).

Brazil and Pix's success

In Brazil, as in many other emerging economies, the growth of digital payments has been driven by the increasing use of smartphones, the growth of e-commerce, and the government's efforts to promote digital payments. The Central Bank of Brazil launched in 2020 a real-time payment system, Pix, that allows users to send and receive money instantly. Pix has been a game changer in Brazil's payment eco system: as of 2024, it had become the most popular payment method, with over 120 million users.

Brazil expects to follow suit with its CBDC, Digital Brazilian Real, or DREX. The Brazilian Central Bank (BCB) is currently in the development stage. The Brazilian CBDC will be an extension of the physical currency, with its value equal to the Brazilian real. It will be based on a blockchain technology inspired by Ethereum (Reuters, 2023[15]). This means that the CBDC will be a digital currency that is secured by cryptography and distributed across a network of computers. The BCB will work with institutions to distribute and run the CBDC. There will be a limit on individual holdings. For the time being, the central bank is focusing on online transactions and domestic use of DREX (Banco Central Do Brasil, 2023[16]). The completion of the pilot phase initially scheduled for 2023 had to be postponed, which may delay the launch of Brazil's CBDC until early 2025 (Economist Intelligence Unit, 2024[17]). While the fast adoption of Pix was remarkable, it remains to be seen whether DREX will manage to do as well.

Looking forward: Potential Impact of CBDCs

Central Bank Digital Currencies (CBDCs) have the potential to impact economies in several ways. While the specific effects will depend on the design and implementation of each CBDC, here are some general ways CBDCs could impact economies:

- **Payment efficiency and financial inclusion**: CBDCs can enhance payment systems, making transactions faster, more secure, and less expensive. They can provide greater financial inclusion by enabling individuals without access to traditional banking services to participate in digital payments and the formal financial system.
- **Monetary policy and central bank control**: CBDCs can offer central banks new tools for implementing monetary policy. With CBDCs, central banks can have more direct control over the

money supply, as they can monitor and influence transactions in real time. This increased control can potentially aid in stabilising the economy and managing inflation.

- **Reduced dependence on intermediaries**: By allowing peer-to-peer transactions, CBDCs may facilitate direct transactions between individuals and businesses, potentially bypassing traditional banking intermediaries. This could impact the role and business models of commercial banks.
- **Data collection and privacy**: CBDCs could provide central banks with access to more comprehensive and real-time transaction data, which can improve economic analysis and policy making. However, the collection and use of such data raise privacy concerns. Striking a balance between data privacy and the benefits of data analysis will be a critical consideration.
- **Cross-border payments and remittances**: CBDCs could simplify and expedite cross-border transactions, reducing costs and settlement times, with positive implications for international trade and remittances, particularly for individuals and businesses in developing countries.
- **Financial stability and systemic risk**: CBDCs may impact the stability of the financial system. On one hand, CBDCs can enhance financial stability by reducing the risks associated with physical cash, such as counterfeiting and illicit activities. On the other hand, if CBDCs lead to significant shifts in deposits from commercial banks to the central bank, it could impact the banking system's stability and liquidity.
- **Technological innovation and digital economy**: The introduction of CBDCs can drive technological innovation in the financial sector and promote the development of digital infrastructure. It may also foster the growth of digital economies and support the integration of new technologies such as smart contracts and programmable money.

The impact of CBDCs will vary across countries, depending on their specific economic structures, financial systems, and policy objectives. A critical factor of success will be the trust of the citizens in their currency and, most importantly, their governments.

The digital revolution offered emerging markets the opportunity to address major problems faced by their payment systems. They seized it. They have been at the forefront of mobile payments and are also more advanced in adopting Central Bank Digital Currencies. Time will tell if this new system helps them enjoy more stable financial systems and advance in financial inclusion and sustainable development.

References

Atlantic Council (n.d.), *Central Bank Digital Currency Tracker*, https://www.atlanticcouncil.org/cbdctracker/ (accessed on 1 March 2024). [9]

Banco Central Do Brasil (2023), *Drex – Digital Brazilian Real*, https://www.bcb.gov.br/en/financialstability/drex_en (accessed on 1 March 2024). [16]

Carapella, F. (2024), *Financial Stability Implications of CBDC*, Federal Reserve Board, Washington, D.C., https://www.federalreserve.gov/econres/feds/files/2024021pap.pdf. [4]

Casanova, L. and A. Miroux (2023), *Emerging Market Multinationals Report 2023: Risks and Realignments*, Cornel S.C. Johnson College of Business, Ithaca, https://doi.org/10.7298/aqwm-7z64. [7]

Economist Intelligence Unit (2024), *Brazil prepares to launch digital currency by early 2025*, https://www.eiu.com/n/brazil-prepares-to-launch-digital-currency-by-early-2025/ (accessed on 1 March 2024). [17]

EOS Intelligence (2024), *eNaira: Is It Here to Stay or Are Nigerians Going to Say 'Nay'?*, https://www.eos-intelligence.com/perspectives/technology/enaira-is-it-here-to-stay-or-are-nigerians-going-to-say-nay/ (accessed on 1 March 2024). [13]

Flemming, J. (2024), *Implications of a U.S. CBDC for International Payments and the Role of the Dollar*, FEDS Notes, Board of Governors of the Federal Reserve System, Washington D.C., https://doi.org/10.17016/2380-7172.3435. [5]

Gandhi, M. (2023), *Future of digital currency in India*, https://www.pwc.in/research-and-insights-hub/future-of-digital-currency-in-india.html (accessed on 1 March 2024). [12]

Jahan, S. (2022), *Towards Central Bank Digital Currencies in Asia and the Pacific: Results of a Regional Survey*, International Monetary Fund, Washington D.C, https://www.imf.org/en/Publications/fintech-notes/Issues/2022/09/27/Towards-Central-Bank-Digital-Currencies-in-Asia-and-the-Pacific-Results-of-a-Regional-Survey-523914. [3]

Ledger Insights (n.d.), *Bahamas Sand Dollar CBDC has $ 2.1m in circulation after 3 years*, https://www.ledgerinsights.com/bahamas-sand-dollar-cbdc-has-2-1m-in-circulation-after-3-years/ (accessed on 1 March 2024). [14]

Mohácsi, P. (2023), *The Digital Economy's New Monetary Imperative*, https://www.project-syndicate.org/onpoint/cbdcs-have-become-a-political-imperative-by-piroska-nagy-mohacsi-2023-06 (accessed on 1 March 2024). [2]

Nambiampurath, R. (2023), *WeChat Pay Integrates Digital Yuan App for Faster Payments*, https://beincrypto.com/wechat-pay-integrated-digital-yuan-app-fast-payments/ (accessed on 1 March 2024). [8]

Prasad, E. (2021), *The Future of Money: How the Digital Revolution Is Transforming Currencies and Finance*, Cambridge, Massachusetts: The Belknap Press of Harvard, https://www.hup.harvard.edu/books/9780674258440. [1]

Reserve Bank of India (2022), *Concept Note on Central Bank Digital Currency*, RBI, Mumbai, https://rbidocs.rbi.org.in/rdocs/PublicationReport/Pdfs/CONCEPTNOTEACB531172E0B4DFC9A6E506C2C24FFB6.PDF. [10]

Reuters (2023), *Brazil central bank names its digital currency "DREX", scheduled for 2024 launch*, https://www.reuters.com/technology/brazil-central-bank-names-its-digital-currency-drex-scheduled-2024-launch-2023-08-07/ (accessed on 1 March 2024). [15]

Singh, A. (2024), *India CBDC Insider Reveals Current Stance of Country's Central Bank*, https://www.coindesk.com/policy/2024/02/02/india-cbdc-insider-reveals-current-stance-of-countrys-central-bank/ (accessed on 1 March 2024). [11]

US Federal Reserve (2022), *Money and Payments: The US Dollar in the Age of Digital Transformation*, Board of Governors of the Federal Reserve, Washington D.C, https://www.federalreserve.gov/publications/files/money-and-payments-20220120.pdf. [6]